YOU GOT THIS!

OTHER TITLES FROM BLOOMSBURY EDUCATION

What Every Teacher Needs to Know: How to embed evidence-informed teaching and learning in your school by Jade Pearce

The Wellbeing Toolkit: Sustaining, supporting and enabling school staff by Andrew Cowley

What Works?: Research and evidence for successful teaching by Lee Elliot Major and Steve Higgins

Teaching Rebooted: Using the science of learning to transform classroom practice by Jon Tait

The Inclusive Classroom: A new approach to differentiation by Daniel Sobel and Sara Alston

Fast Feedback: How one primary school abolished written marking by Lesley Hill with Gemma Whitby

YOU GOT THIS!

Thriving as an early career teacher with Mr T

Andrew Taylor

BLOOMSBURY EDUCATION

LONDON OXFORD NEW YORK NEW DELHI SYDNEY

BLOOMSBURY EDUCATION
Bloomsbury Publishing Plc
50 Bedford Square, London, WC1B 3DP, UK
29 Earlsfort Terrace, Dublin 2, Ireland

BLOOMSBURY, BLOOMSBURY EDUCATION and the Diana logo are trademarks
of Bloomsbury Publishing Plc

First published in the UK 2023 by Bloomsbury Publishing Plc
This edition published in the UK 2023 by Bloomsbury Publishing Plc

A catalogue record for this book is available from the British Library

ISBN: PB: 978-1-8019-9019-6; ePDF: 978-1-8019-9020-2; ePub: 978-1-8019-9017-2

2 4 6 8 10 9 7 5 3 1 (paperback)

Text design by Marcus Duck Design
Typeset by Newgen KnowledgeWorks Pvt. Ltd., Chennai, India
Printed and bound in the UK by CPI Group (UK) Ltd, Croydon, CR0 4YY

To find out more about our authors and books visit www.bloomsbury.com
and sign up for our newsletters

This book is dedicated to the amazing NQTs I have mentored.

BS, MC, AM, JT, TA, MB, SH, MS, JN, HB, CR, CB, GD, LF, LB, ES, LM

Each one of you has shaped the mentor, teacher and person I am today.

To LG, PE and EJP – your belief in me and the opportunities you gave have led me to where I am now. Thank you.

Finally, to Mrs T and the little Ts – your love and support is invaluable and I could not do what I do without you beside me.

CONTENTS

HOW TO USE THIS BOOK

This book is here to help you. Much like the work I do on Twitter, it is full of advice, tips and strategies to help you to thrive as you embark on your teaching career. I wanted to create a book that, at various points in your teaching career (or teacher training), you could take from the shelf to guide and reassure you. It is based on my experiences, and whilst I recognise that every teacher and school is different, and that difference should be celebrated, hopefully there will be plenty in here that can support you in your practice.

The book is organised into chapters that focus on key priorities for early career teachers (ECTs) and in a way that should help you to quickly navigate and find the information that you need. The book can be read chronologically, but I have written it in a way that means you can dip in and out of it depending on the area on which you are looking for advice. Each chapter contains the following features:

Daily tip

The daily tips are taken straight from my work on Twitter. In 2018, I set up my Twitter account, @MrTs_NQTs, as for the previous ten years I had been working as an NQT mentor and over that time I had seen that the support I was offering to NQTs was not always replicated elsewhere. I wanted to develop a place where NQTs and ECTs could seek advice, ask questions and receive support to help them to navigate their early career.

Chapter introduction

Each of the chapter introductions briefly describes the topics/areas that will be covered. These are intended to help you to quickly navigate to the area of interest.

Coaching moment

Within each chapter you will find coaching moments to help you to reflect on where you are in your current journey and to think about where you need to go next.

Thoughts from an ECT

You will find the thoughts and experiences of other ECTs near the end of each chapter. It is important to me that the voices of ECTs are amplified, and I hugely recognise what ECTs have to offer the profession and the support and reassurance that they can offer to each other.

Key takeaway

The key takeaway at the end of each chapter provides a summary of the key points discussed for you to consider before moving onto the next chapter.

The book was written keeping the Early Career Framework (ECF; DfE, 2019) in mind. The ECF was devised to provide a consistency in access to CPD for those in their early teaching career, and the concepts and ideas that it presents are there to give you a strong foundation on which to build your career. You will notice overlaps and similarities in some of the areas, as I wanted to ensure that this book would support you in thriving during your ECT induction.

I hope that you enjoy reading it and that it helps you to navigate your journey in teaching. Let me know what you think and come and find me at @MrTs_NQTs on Twitter.

I also want to take this opportunity to say congratulations. Whatever stage of your teaching career you are at, you are making a huge difference and a positive impact on the lives of the pupils that you teach. You should be hugely proud of what you have chosen to do and the difference that you are making every day.

I hope that there is something in this book that can help, reassure or inspire you to be the best teacher that you are capable of being. Remember that there is only one you, and that your journey in teaching is uniquely yours.

Remember, your best will always be good enough.

#YouGotThis

Mr T

CHAPTER 1
SECURING YOUR FIRST TEACHING ROLE

Mr T's NQT/ECT support
@MrTs_NQTs

Daily tip

If you get called for an interview, make sure you contact the school to accept! Read the guidance you have been sent thoroughly to make sure that on the day you are equipped with everything you need.

In this chapter we will:

➡ Explore the process of securing your first post, from the search to accepting the job.

➡ Understand the process of how to find the right school for you.

➡ Consider the best way in which to write a personal statement that sells you as an individual.

➡ Explore the interview process and potential tasks and questions.

Securing your first post can be a real rollercoaster of emotions, but it is the gateway into your career. Securing your first teaching job can be an intense process and interviews don't always give you the chance to show everything that you are capable of. Personally I don't interview well, and getting the opportunity to show what I am capable of, without feeling the intense glare of an interview panel, is not always easy. This chapter will help to guide you through the whole process, from finding the school that you want to apply for, right through to saying yes when you are offered the job!

Finding the right school

Schools can advertise their vacancies in a variety of ways. Some will advertise on their own websites, some will advertise through the local authority website and others use local job search websites or national teacher websites, such as eteach, TES and the DfE's teaching vacancies website:

https://teaching-vacancies.service.gov.uk

Independent schools may even advertise in the local press.

You may find yourself in the position of living on the cusp of different authorities, or you may be uncertain as to whether you want to work where you trained or to head back home. The best advice is to set up alerts on the websites for where you envisage teaching – this will give you a sense of what different schools are like and which ones will be the right fit for you to start your teaching career in.

If you find a school that you want to apply to, the next step is to trawl through their website and find out as much as you can about them. Look at the school's values – do they align with yours? What do their policies tell you about what their expectations are for staff and children? What is the best thing about the school, and does that fit with what you value about education? I also find that newsletters to parents always make interesting reading and can show you the real priorities for the school. Do you know anyone who works there, or have you had a fellow trainee that has been on placement there? Remember that you are choosing a school to support you in your induction and early career. Make sure that it is the right one.

Next up, make contact! Use the contact details shared in the advert, get in touch with the school and use the opportunity to find out more about the role and, ideally, to arrange a tour of the school and/or have a chat with the headteacher. This contact is important to help you to get a sense of whether or not you see yourself fitting in at the school. Schools will also want to get to know you and see whether you are the right fit for them. Crucially, though, this is also a great time for you to decide whether it is a school in which you want to work, because finding the right school for you is so important.

When visiting a school, questions to ask yourself include: What is the environment like? What are the children doing? What are the staff doing? How are the children interacting with the person showing you around? Does the school give you the feeling of 'I could be happy here'? However, it can be tricky at times to visit a school when the children are there, and going after school can be just as beneficial. On this occasion, questions to consider include: Are teachers chatting jovially in the corridors or are they surrounded by barricades of books in the classrooms? Is the car park clearing by 4.30 pm or are staff hard at work at 6.00 pm? This is not to advocate any of these ways of working – every school is different, and three people can walk around the same school and get a different feeling about it. Remember that finding the right school for you is so important (have I mentioned that yet?!).

When you do call or visit, listen carefully to what you are being told. Headteachers love to talk about their schools, so pay attention. Don't feel that you have to go armed with a list of questions (especially ones to which you can find the answer on the school's website) and don't try to tell them all about how amazing you are. It is your chance to find out about the school. If the head wants to know more about you, they will ask you. If you do spot things that interest you as you are going around, ask a question about those things. It shows that you are listening and taking it all in. There is never an expectation for you to ask a question; sometimes when showing people around I can spot the candidates who are just waiting to ask a question and aren't taking things in at all. I also heard a story where one candidate elbowed another out of the way so that they could walk next to the headteacher – don't be that person! Schools are interested in employing a person who will fit in, just as much as they are interested in how good they are at teaching. On the day, if there is close competition between two candidates, they will always choose the person who is the right fit for the school. Schools can help anyone to develop as a teacher – but they are not equipped to perform personality transplants!

COACHING MOMENT

- ▶ What type of school best suits you as a person and as a teacher?
  - ▶ Do you enjoy working as part of a planning team?
  - ▶ Do you prefer having free reign to plan the way you want to?
  - ▶ Do you want to be in a large multi-form-entry school?
  - ▶ Would you prefer to be in a smaller village school?
  - ▶ How far are you happy to commute?
  - ▶ Would living close to the school put you off?

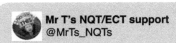 

Mr T's NQT/ECT support
@MrTs_NQTs

Don't be flattered into accepting a job that doesn't feel right. Schools may offer you a job without a formal interview or, even after an interview, overwhelm you with positive feedback. If the school doesn't feel right, don't feel obliged to accept.

Applying for the role

Now that you have found the right school and you want to apply, it will be time to complete the application form.

Most schools will ask for you to complete the application form as your way of applying. There is no standard format – each school will want the same information but may present it differently. This makes applying time-consuming – make sure that you are applying for a job you would accept!

Some schools may ask for an application form and a covering letter and, on a very rare occasion (usually if recruiting through an agent or if it is an independent school), a school may ask for a CV and a covering letter. An example CV layout can be found at the end of this chapter.

Regardless of what they ask for, you will need to craft a personal statement. This is often the biggest section of the application form. Writing a personal statement is your chance to sell yourself and show what you have done and what you can do.

Nearly every job advert will have a person specification (or spec); this is your guide – your structure, if you will. In theory, if you demonstrate all the elements of the person spec, the school will call you for interview. However, if they receive 40 applications for one job that all meet the person spec, it will be the depth at which you meet the requirements that will determine whether or not you are invited for interview.

If there is no person spec, then make sure you cover the fundamentals when completing the application form and writing your personal statement:

> behaviour management

> working with colleagues

> safeguarding

> your views on effective teaching and learning – share the best lesson that you have ever taught

> how you promote progress for all pupils

> contributions to the wider school

> you as a person – hobbies and interests.

All applicants will talk about how they have taught lessons, how they have developed behaviour management skills and how they contributed to the wider school life; the applicants who stand out are those who can demonstrate impact. If you have utilised specific approaches during lessons you have taught, why did you use that approach and what was the impact on the learners? You've devised your own behaviour management system; what was the impact on pupil behaviour and on your practice going forward? Giving specific examples and being able to demonstrate impact shows that you are reflective and that you have ownership of your own development.

Demonstrate how you will add value to the school. When you've visited the school or scoured the website, use the information that you have gained to show that you understand the school and how you would find your place in it. For example, the school may currently be focusing on diversity and representation in the curriculum. If you have had experience of this or have a keen interest in the area, convey this through your application. Equally, if you have a skill or interest that sits outside of what the school currently offers, then make it clear how you would be willing to use this to develop the provision for the school. For example, if you are a keen gardener and would be willing to set up and establish a gardening club with children, this would show how you can add to the 'extensive range of extracurricular provision' that the school currently offers.

Personalise your application to each school. This may seem obvious, but the person spec for most teaching jobs and schools is pretty much identical. This means that you can reuse examples from your experience. However, always proofread before submitting. If you include the wrong school's name in your application form, chances are it will end up on the 'no' pile! Personalise your application by drawing on information that you have seen on the website. If you have visited or contacted the school, take time to mention this and thank them for showing you around, identifying something that you particularly remember or took note of. Taking the time to show that you know the school goes a long way. Where possible, don't see it as just a top-and-tail personalisation – try to weave the links to the school throughout. For example, when you talk about the way in which you manage behaviour, show how it would complement or align with the school's behaviour policy.

Sometimes it can be tricky to know how to start. You could try something along the lines of 'I have chosen to apply to [name of school] because I can see from your school website and having had the chance to visit your school that...' or 'Having visited [name of school] and from looking at your website, I can see that this would be a school that would nurture and develop me as a teacher in my early career'. You can then go on to talk about what has given you that opinion, how it is that you have reached the idea that this is the best place for you and why you are applying.

Make sure that you talk about you as a person. What do you like to do in your spare time? How do you ensure that you have time to rest and recover? This is a chance to also share your personality. What kind of a person are you? What are your character strengths that will help you to be part of a team? Remember that schools employ people, just as much as they employ teachers. It is important that a school can see that you will 'fit in', and if you haven't had the chance to visit, this is your opportunity to show them that you will.

Your application form is also a chance to share any career aspirations. Where do you see yourself in five years' time? Are there specific subjects in which you have an interest that you may want to lead or take responsibility for? Again, it will give the school a sense of who you are and will be an opportunity for them to think about how they might be able to best support you.

The best applications that I read are those where I can visualise the teacher in the class and get a sense of them just by reading their application, through the specific examples they have shared with clear impact and reflection.

Keep your personal statement to a maximum of two sides of A4. That way it will fit as part of an application form or, if a school does ask for a CV and covering letter, you can use your personal statement for that. If a school asks for an application form and a covering letter or email, the covering letter would be the part that is most personalised to the school, demonstrating what you believe they can offer you and what you, in turn, would add to the school. The personal statement would demonstrate the person spec but may be less personalised to the school. Remember to give examples and show impact.

Proofread, proofread and proofread again! Checking for simple errors or issues with grammar can make all the difference to an application form. It demonstrates your subject knowledge if it is well written (or not), and it shows that you take genuine care about what you do. If you find it hard to spot errors in your own writing, ask a 'critical friend' to look through it and provide you with honest feedback.

Finally, get it in on time! It doesn't matter how early you submit it, but it is important that you meet the deadline. It shows good organisation and time management. If for some reason you spot an advert close to the application deadline, make contact and explain that you have only just seen the vacancy; they may have a bit of wiggle room in the deadline. Sometimes, getting the right people together to shortlist can take a while.

The rest of the application form will be a list of qualifications and previous employment. Schools will have staff who are trained in safer recruitment and they will look for gaps in employment since leaving education. If you know there are gaps for any reason (maternity leave, travelling, etc.), try to explain these in your application form. If you don't, schools have a duty of care to ask you about the reason for the gaps.

Then begins the wait! Most schools will have a date by which if you have not heard it means that you have been unsuccessful. Others will contact you by a certain date to let you know that you have been unsuccessful. You are entitled to ask for feedback about your application if you are not successful, but bear in mind that it may sometimes be simply because of the number of applications that a school receives. Schools in popular areas, or that have a good reputation within the community, can easily receive upwards of 50 applications for one class teacher job. The most that I have ever heard of for one job is over 100 applications – this is why it is so important that you present yourself as professionally as you can on paper.

COACHING MOMENT

▶ What is your unique selling point? Is this emphasised enough in your application?

▶ What experiences have had the most profound impact on you as a teacher?

▶ When you read back your supporting statement, does it sound like you? Or could it be for any teacher?

 **Daily tip**

 **Mr T's NQT/ECT support**
@MrTs_NQTs

If you're applying for a job in a year group that you haven't taught before, but in a school you want to work in, talk about how your experiences will support you. For example, having taught Year 2, I would use this knowledge to ensure that pupils in Year 1 are where they need to be.

♡   ↻   ♡   ↑

The interview

You have now secured an interview! Most schools will give you at least 48 hours' notice before the interview. (It can be shorter than this if another applicant withdraws late in the process.)

When you receive an email or telephone call to notify you that you have been successful and invited to interview, you will need to formally confirm your attendance. Make sure that you do this so that the school can prepare for your arrival and ensure that you get the full information needed for the interview.

Every school's interview process will be slightly different. However, there will be some certainties. You will have to provide ID on the day and sometimes proof of qualifications before starting the interview process. Make sure you remember to bring along everything that the school has asked you to. And double-check this!

■ Tips for the day

You will need to be at the school for a certain time, so make sure you have a dry run in rush hour traffic, just to make sure that you leave yourself enough time. If it is a virtual interview, log on with time to spare, double-check that your technology is working and give yourself plenty of time to get it sorted if it is not!

Dress professionally – always go as formal as you can (you don't need to wear a ball gown or a tuxedo, but a smart suit would be advisable). This is also the case if you are online. Don't just smarten up the top half – go fully smartly dressed. You may get asked to fetch something, and you don't want to be in your pyjamas and bunny slippers!

You will be nervous; it is to be expected and it shows that you care. The panel know you will be nervous so don't worry about it. Use your nervous energy to help you to get through the day and help you to deliver a dynamic performance. I can assure you that the panel will be nervous too. They want to appoint the best person for their school.

When you arrive at the school you will no doubt be greeted by the school secretary. This is your chance to make a positive impression on the wider school team. All staff in a school are vitally important and will have an influence over the outcome of the interview. Be friendly and polite to everyone. Remember, the school is looking for someone who will fit in with the team. Equally, if you see children around the school, smile and greet them; it goes a long way.

The sense of professionalism that you need to display will be in effect from the moment that you pull into the car park to the time that you are well on your way home.

■ What to expect on the day

Now to the nitty gritty – what you can expect on the day.

They will want to see you teach!

Every school is different in what information they might share with you regarding this. Some may be very prescriptive: 'You have 20 minutes to teach a maths lesson on place value to Year 2 students.' Others may give you some choice: 'You can teach either a 30-minute maths or English session on the subject of your choice to a group of Year 3 pupils.' Or perhaps: 'The current topic is senses; please plan and teach a 30-minute lesson for a group of Year 1 pupils.' Or you may even have: 'You have 30 minutes with a group of Year 6 children. Please teach a lesson that will show you at your best.' Recently, some schools have not shared the focus for teaching with the applicants beforehand but have given them a focus and time to prepare on the day. Whatever the brief is, stick to it!

Always play to your strengths. I often get asked for tips for interview lessons or ideas of what to do. I could suggest a full puppet show to demonstrate the importance of the use of parenthesis in writing; that would be right up my street, but may send others into a cold sweat. We are each individual teachers and have areas with which we are confident. Start with something that you know or an aspect that resonates with you. As part of the interview, you will often be asked to justify why you chose a specific activity or approach – 'because Mr T suggested it' would not be an acceptable answer. Ownership of anything you teach is so important.

Whatever you choose, this is the time to show them what you are made of. Schools are looking for how you have chosen to structure the learning, the activities and the opportunities for children. More importantly, though, they want to see how you connect with the children. How do you manage behaviour? How do you adapt when things don't go the way that you expect? How do you develop a rapport with the children and a TA (if you have one in the lesson)? Twenty or 30 minutes isn't long, but you will be asked to reflect on the lesson as part of your panel interview, and this can be your chance to show how it would fit into a learning journey and to talk about where you would take children next. Please make sure that you introduce yourself at the start of the session – so often candidates don't, and it gets a bit awkward for the children when they want your attention.

Schools may provide you with additional information about the class that you will be teaching – how many pupils have SEND (special educational needs and disability), EAL (English as an additional language), etc. – but some schools won't. If you want to find out more, make contact with the school and they will happily provide further information about the class. Try to write one email or make one phone call and ask all your questions in one go. Keep in mind that the more you know, the more they will expect to see you accommodate. If there are specific resources that you want to use, either make sure that you can source them yourself or double-check that the school has them. Not all schools will have Numicon, for example, so check before you start planning. The worst thing in the world is when a candidate turns up and asks for equipment that we don't have, and you can see them visibly start to panic. With that in mind, make sure that you have multiple copies of any electronic presentations you have, preferably saved in different formats. Again, you don't want to be scuppered by the outdated tech in the school! Access on Google Drive or OneDrive may also be useful but, again, some of these can be blocked by a school's filtering systems. Finally, if you want paper copies of activities for children, where possible get them printed beforehand. If this isn't possible, make sure that you arrive at the school early enough to copy them or have a plan B up your sleeve – just in case that is the day the photocopier decides to blow up!

The other guaranteed part of the interview process will be the panel interview. There will be at least three people in the panel interview; at least one will have safer recruitment training to ensure the duty of care for children, and most likely one will be a school governor. Chances are that you will be asked to feed back on how your lesson went earlier in the day. Be honest and reflective – if you feel that it was a car crash, admit it, but be factual about why you feel that. The worst thing that you can do is say that it is the best lesson you have ever taught if it did not go at all well. Schools want to see that you can reflect accurately and honestly.

■ The panel interview

The panel interview can be a time where your nerves get the better of you. If you know that your hands shake or you start to fidget, just gently move your hands under the table and press your thumb and index finger pads together. This can get you back in the moment and gives your body something physical to focus on.

When asked a question, take your time to respond. Pause before answering and if you find yourself getting lost in your answer about halfway through, ask them to repeat the question so that you feel happy with how you have answered.

The time when candidates appear most relaxed and in control is when they speak about lived experiences. Try to have pre-prepared examples of how you have managed behaviour successfully, your best lesson, when you have worked as part of a team, when you have acted on advice and when you have actively developed your own practice. These can give you focal points around which to wrap your answers. Speaking from experience always gives confidence.

The questions that you may be asked will vary depending on school priorities, but you will certainly be asked a question on safeguarding. Here is a selection of other questions that you may be asked. Whenever answering a question, draw on your own examples from your experience and demonstrate how you have 'lived' your answer.

> What can we do as a school to help you to thrive in your first year with us?

> If you were finding something tricky, what steps would you take?

> What would you as a person add to our school?

> If I were to walk around the school, how would I know that I had entered your classroom?

> What, for you, has been the teaching approach that has had the biggest impact on your practice?

> Which of your behaviour management strategies has had the biggest impact on pupil behaviour?

> What, for you, is the most important thing that children will learn in your class?

> How would you ensure that children have a smooth transition into your class?

> What makes you an inspirational teacher?

> What does the term 'safeguarding' mean to you?

> How do you ensure that you meet the needs of all pupils in your class?

> An unhappy parent demands to speak to you as you are welcoming the children into the classroom. How do you deal with this?

> Tell us about the best lesson that you have taught. How do you know that it was good? What did you do that made it successful?

> How would you respond to feedback from a member of the SLT with whom you disagreed?

> How would you handle a dispute about your teaching with your experienced teaching assistant?

> How would a child know that they were safe in your class?

> What is the biggest challenge that you have faced and how did you overcome it?

> If we didn't offer you the job, what would we be missing out on?

This is not an exhaustive list, but it will give you a good flavour of what to expect. If you search for #MrTsIQ on Twitter, a whole raft of potential questions will appear.

Another question that you may be asked is about your strengths and weaknesses. Try to avoid the word 'weakness' in your answer. Discuss an area for development and possibly link to something that you have not had much experience of yet, but that you are hoping to develop. You could also discuss the steps that you have taken to develop yourself in that area already. Be prepared that there could be a random question! We wanted to get a sense of personality when interviewing one year, so we asked the candidates: 'If we were to put on a staff pantomime, which panto character would you be and why?' – it lifted the mood and gave a real sense of people's personalities.

At the end of the panel interview, you will be offered the chance to ask any questions. You may have a question; you may not. Your question may have been answered during the day; if it has, articulate this to the panel. If you aren't already aware, you should ask about the provision and support for ECTs. The best question that I ever got asked by a candidate was: 'What do you think is the best thing about working here?' That would help you to get a sense of the people and a personal view of the school. Remember that finding the right school for you is so important (have I mentioned that yet?!).

Daily tip

Mr T's NQT/ECT support
@MrTs_NQTs

Remember that even after the formal part of the interview ends, you are still being interviewed. Remain professional until you are fully off the premises.

■ Other tasks on the day

Along with the formal interview and the teaching task, on the interview day you may be asked to have an interview with the school council – be prepared for anything! Definitely have a child-friendly joke up your sleeve, such as: 'How do you make an octopus laugh? Give it ten-tickles.' If children have designed the questions, they could be anything, from 'If you were an animal what would you be?' to 'How will you make sure that I am safe in school?'

There may also be tasks for the day.

You may be asked to present to a small panel. It will most likely be about you and something about which you feel confident talking – for example, a presentation on your best lesson, or what your values and ethos for education are. Again, stick to the brief and double-check that you have everything with you!

Alternatively, you may be asked to engage in a subject knowledge task – for example, you may be asked to complete a previous Year 6 SATs paper or GCSE paper for secondary, or to write about yourself or your journey to becoming a teacher, where they can check your written language skills.

There may be a marking or assessment task. You could be given a piece of writing to level or provide feedback on for children (especially if you are applying for a Year 6 or Year 2 job). Equally, you may be given a set of data for a class and be asked to identify the next steps for children.

You may also be given a planning task. This could involve being given a book or theme as a stimulus and being asked to plan a series of lessons across the curriculum that would be inspired by the stimulus with which you have been provided.

Another possibility is that there could be an 'in tray' or 'desktop' task, such as writing a response to a parental concern, or a letter of introduction to your class or the parents, or even having to deal with a safeguarding concern and explaining, in written form, how you would follow it up. Please remember that any written tasks will be checked for subject knowledge – make sure that you proofread what you have written.

Keep in mind that any tasks that are unseen and introduced on the day will be unseen for everyone.

The entire day is about the school getting to know you and seeing whether you are the right fit for them. Above all else, a headteacher will be thinking, 'Will they fit in my school?' and 'Will they enhance or complement what I have already?', as well as, 'Can I support them and will I be able to work with that person?'.

At the very end of the day, you will be asked: 'If we were to offer you the job, would you accept?' Always answer 'yes' at this point – it gives you time to decide. If you hesitate, you may cast a seed of doubt in the interviewer's mind and it may jeopardise the chances of them offering you the post. The school will also want to confirm the best contact number for you so that they can get in touch with you later that day. This is one of the best things about teacher interviews; you normally find out whether you have been successful on the same day. If you are successful, they will contact you and let you know.

Once the person who has been successful has been contacted, the school will then contact those candidates who have been unsuccessful. If you happen to be unsuccessful, you are entitled to feedback. Schools may provide feedback there and then, or they may ask for an alternative time when they can speak to you.

Whatever the outcome of the day, if you did your best, you can walk away proud. You are looking for the right school for you, and there is a school out there that is looking for you too! Sometimes it can take a while to find each other. Be true to yourself and give it your all, and you can always be proud of what you have achieved.

COACHING MOMENT

- ▶ Have you planned a lesson that shows your strengths? Why have you chosen that approach?
- ▶ If asked about your unique selling point, what would you say?
- ▶ Have you given yourself the best chance of securing the job by having everything ready, organised and prepared?
- ▶ What examples of your own effective practice can you consider before going to interview? What have been your key moments in teaching so far?

Thoughts from an ECT

I'll be honest, I didn't follow the advice of my lecturers when securing my PGCE – I did what felt right for me. Having an interview after teaching a total of three full lessons was not what I expected, but I knew that this was the best time for me because this was when I was more likely to take the advice of my mentor and was more willing to try new things. I interviewed for my ECT position in December, after only starting to take small sections of lessons in November. I was lucky in that I was interviewing in a new city where I didn't know anybody – I really had nothing to lose. This was the attitude that I went into my interview with, and it was the factor that helped my success – I was so calm and collected, which, if you ask my PGCE mentor, did not follow for the rest of my PGCE!

If you have been invited to interview, the biggest thing to remember is that you are good enough to be there. It doesn't matter how experienced the other candidates are – you don't know what that school is looking for. They may be looking for a new teacher who they can integrate into a developing department. This is what happened with me; I was up against very experienced candidates, but my school wanted a new teacher who they could help to develop. This is a good bit of advice; I applied for a new school that is still developing its identity and culture. As an ECT, at this school I have been able to get involved in discussions that ECTs would not normally be able to, and to take opportunities that, in older, more established schools, would only be open for more experienced staff. Look for a school where you can get involved and develop the other aspects of your career – for me this was a new-build academy. This is something that you can look for before applying by reading the school's development plan, which should be on their website, or by asking the question at interview.

Having the attitude that I didn't have anything to lose helped me massively – as trainee teachers and ECTs, we are often perfectionists, but I saw this as a chance to go and teach in a different setting and to look at how other schools do things. And an hour after leaving, I had secured my position.

There is obviously preparation that you will need to do, but this is more practical and will be dependent on your setting and subject. Carry out a practice lesson and interview in your placement; this will help you to walk in knowing that you are a subject expert and that you are a fantastic teacher; otherwise you wouldn't be there.

Good luck and remember that the interview is just as much about you finding out whether the school is right for your career and development as it is about the school working out whether you are right for them.

Hatty Ruddick, Secondary Business Studies ECT

Key takeaways

- Finding the right school for you is so important.

- When applying for schools, show how you know the school and that you have made an informed decision to apply.

- Spend time on your personal statement showing you as a teacher, and make sure that you demonstrate the impact that you have had.

- When called for interview, make sure that you always remain professional and be true to yourself.

- Schools employ people for who they are as much as they employ them for the teacher that they are.

Example CV format

MR T
1 Taylors Lane, Sometown, SM1 7WN
Email: Mrt.nqts@gmail.com
Contact number: 12345 678912

PERSONAL SUMMARY

I am a committed, passionate, reliable and highly motivated teacher, with a commitment to all learners achieving their potential. I have taught the full primary age range but the majority of my teaching has been in Key Stage 1. I am an effective communicator, who strives to inspire pupils to achieve the best that they can.

My educational philosophy is that teachers are facilitators who provide the opportunities, environment and skills for pupils to thrive.

EDUCATION/QUALIFICATIONS

FROM – TO University of…

FROM – TO Sixth-form college

A levels:

FROM – TO High school

10 GCSEs (including maths and English at grade C+)

EMPLOYMENT HISTORY

Sept 2021 – Aug 2022: Class teacher, This School

- Day-to-day teaching
- Planning, assessing and reporting on pupil progress
- Upholding Safeguarding and Health and Safety policies and processes
- Supervision of pupils at playtime
- Running Food Club and Tennis Club

TRAINING

Safeguarding training (September 2021)

Read Write Inc. training (2021)

INTERESTS

I regularly play tennis and enjoy reading and family time with my wife and two children.

REFERENCES

One would usually be your university tutor – they will guide you on who you should put down. Most universities hold references centrally, so make sure that you double-check who the request needs to go to.

Name and contact details of a headteacher from a placement school – make sure that you ask them first.

CHAPTER 2

WHAT TO EXPECT FROM YOUR ECT INDUCTION

Mr T's NQT/ECT support
@MrTs_NQTs

ECTs, it is important you know the expectations of you for your ECT induction, and also the expectations you should have for your school and appropriate body. This document 'Induction for early career teachers (England)' (DfE, 2021) will tell you everything you need to know. It's an easy read too! #YouGotThis

In this chapter we will:

➡ Explore the two strands of your induction: the ECF and ECT induction.

➡ Identify the processes involved in induction.

➡ Look at how you can get the most out of the induction process.

This chapter will focus on the expectations that you should have for your induction in your first and second year of teaching and how to get the most out of the process.

Your ECT induction

The following diagram highlights the difference between the Early Career Framework (ECF) and your Early Career Teacher (ECT) induction. Whilst they occur at the same time, they are separate processes.

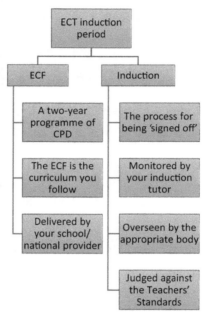

As we move from the old ways of NQT induction, there is still much confusion around the new Early Career Framework (ECF) and Early Career Teacher (ECT) induction. We will look at each in its own right, because whilst they occur at the same time, they are not interdependent.

The Early Career Framework

In recognition of the poor retention rates in early career teachers (30 per cent of teachers leaving within the first five years of their career – DfE, 2016), the DfE have invested in a curriculum to support teachers in their first two years of teaching. The Early Career Framework (ECF) (DfE, 2019) outlines what you should be 'taught' during your CPD in the first two years of your career. It groups content into Professional Behaviours, Assessment, Pedagogy, Managing Behaviour and Curriculum. These link closely to the Teachers' Standards; however, it is not a way for you to demonstrate that you are meeting the Teachers' Standards.

Your school will have decided how they will deliver the ECF materials to you. There are three possible scenarios:

> The school will use the ECF to devise and deliver its own CPD.

> The school will use the materials that have been developed by one of the DfE-approved delivery partners.

> The school will sign you up with a delivery partner, who will deliver the materials to you.

There are funding implications for schools, and the final option provides the greatest level of funding for the school and will probably be the favoured option for the majority of schools.

Each provider's materials have been DfE-approved and meet the full requirements of the ECF. However, each provider will deliver the materials in their own way.

One provider may disseminate materials through an online hub for you to access, whilst others may arrange more face-to-face delivery sessions. Whichever provider is used, it will meet the requirements of the ECF.

What is important is your engagement with the ECF. These materials have been developed to support you in your continued professional development. They will align to the key areas of the ECF:

> Professional Behaviours

> Behaviour Management

> Curriculum

> Pedagogy

> Assessment.

These materials will also be a spiral curriculum; at first there may be an overlap with your initial teacher training, but the content will then build in complexity. The later materials need to ensure that you have a clear grasp of the early content to build on.

If a school is delivering a provider's material, how they deliver it is up to the school, but the content will be the same. If a school chooses to develop and deliver their own materials linked to the ECF, this will be bespoke to your school; but, again, the same content will be covered.

Regardless of the approach, receiving ECF training is part of your entitlement as an ECT. You will receive ten per cent additional non-contact time in your first year and five per cent in your second year to engage with these materials. The most common structure is:

> You will have access to the focus of the materials.

> You will have a low-stakes, short observation by your mentor, based on the weekly focus.

> You will then meet with your mentor during your ECT time to discuss feedback and plan next steps.

> There will then be materials from your provider with which to engage to support your development in each area.

Outside of this, the rest of your ECT time should be used to provide opportunities for you to develop as a teacher. These could relate to wider areas of focus linked to induction (we will discuss this later in the chapter) or could link with a school priority. For example, you may be asked to observe a lead practitioner in the school demonstrating a particular approach, or conduct a learning walk to explore a range of approaches to questioning.

You will have a named mentor who will be there to support you with the ECF. Their role is to provide close-to-practice support through low-stakes observation and focused coaching and mentoring, provide CPD, and provide access to and help you to navigate the ECF materials. Their role is not to make any judgements of you in relation to the Teachers' Standards, but to help to deliver the ECF curriculum, support and guide you.

There should be no expectation for you to collate evidence, beyond what you engage with during your ECT time, in order to demonstrate your engagement with the ECF materials.

COACHING MOMENT

▶ How will you access the ECF materials?

▶ Which provider is your school using?

▶ When will you meet with your mentor?

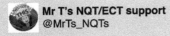

Mr T's NQT/ECT support
@MrTs_NQTs

Daily tip

Your induction tutor will be completing your first review form at Christmas. It is important you have your say. There will be a box on the form for you to share your views. Take the time to fill it in.

Induction

During your first two years in teaching, you will be in your induction period. This time is to support you in your continued development as a teacher, and at the end of the second year a recommendation will be made as to whether you have successfully demonstrated and met the Teachers' Standards.

You will be appointed an induction tutor, who will support you with your induction, and their role is to:

> provide access to CPD

> provide you with a named contact at the appropriate body (either the local authority or a teaching school hub)

> formally observe you (approximately once a half-term)

> carry out progress review meetings at the end of the autumn and spring terms in your first and second year

> carry out formal review meetings at the end of the first and second year

> make a judgement of your performance against the Teachers' Standards

> make a recommendation to the appropriate body at the end of the second year as to whether or not you have successfully completed your induction.

This role should sit alongside the mentor role, and the recommendation is that these roles should be held by different people in the school (although in small schools this can be a challenge).

This is a really positive step based on my experience. Having been an NQT mentor for years and holding both of these responsibilities combined in that role, it can be tough. Every year I would be honest with my NQTs and tell them that I was there to support them. Yes, I would be making a recommendation at the end of the year about whether they had met the standards, but I was also the person who could provide them with the most support. Of the 17 NQTs that I mentored, 16 cried on me at some point in the year, and often it would be because things had deteriorated for them and they had not reached out for support for fear of judgement.

Separating out these roles provides clarity about where both parties sit, the responsibilities that they hold and how they can support you effectively.

During your first few weeks at the school, the induction tutor will meet with you to review your Career Entry Development Profile (CEDP) – or equivalent, depending on what your training provider chooses to call it – to look at the strengths and areas for development that have come out of your training. Your induction tutor will have a wider remit than your mentor, and whilst you are working your way through the ECF, there may be other areas of priority for you and your induction tutor will arrange support to develop these.

Your induction tutor will observe you frequently (about once per half-term) and they will also carry out progress reviews with you each term. These reviews are to discuss the strengths and continued areas of development linked to the Teachers' Standards. At these meetings, you may be asked to share or talk through examples from your practice – planning or marking, for example. You should not be collating this evidence in a folder; it will be captured by your induction tutor in the progress review forms.

Point 2.53 of the statutory induction guidance (DfE, 2021, p. 22) makes this clear:

> 'Evidence for assessments must be drawn from the ECT's work as a teacher during their induction. To ensure evidence gathering is not burdensome for the ECT, formal assessment meetings should be informed by evidence gathered during progress reviews and assessment periods leading up to the formal assessment. This will consist of existing documents and working documents. There is no need for the ECT to create anything new for the formal assessment, they should draw from their work as a teacher and from their induction programme.'

Collating evidence in a folder is an unnecessary burden, and so many ECTs/ NQTs that I hear from have been asked to create folders for evidence that are never even looked at.

More recently, the DfE (2022) have produced further guidance that makes this really clear:

> 'Your induction tutor may ask you to provide evidence of meeting the teachers' standards during your formal assessments. This should only consist of existing documents, such as lesson plans or feedback from observations. There's no need for you to create anything new for a formal assessment.'

At the end of each year, your induction tutor will submit a formal assessment form that will be sent to the appropriate body. At the end of the first year, this will detail your progress against the Teachers' Standards. At the end of the second year, the same form will be used, but you will also receive a recommendation that you have successfully met the Teachers' Standards.

This form will outline your development against the Teachers' Standards, your future targets and the support offered. Whatever is written in this report should not be a surprise to you. You should be kept aware of your progress against the Teachers' Standards throughout your induction. If you feel that there is a lack of transparency and that your mentor or induction tutor are not being clear with their concerns, speak to them about this.

There is also a space on the assessment form for you to record your thoughts and provide your own comments about your progress and the report that has been written about you, and to confirm that you have received your entitlement to the ECF and the statutory entitlements. It is so important that you have your say. I know that for so many staff at appropriate bodies this is the first box they read, and they want to hear your voice coming through.

If you are unsure what to write, consider:

> Is the report accurate?

> Has the support been effective?

> What has been the stand-out moment of your induction so far?

> Has there been a particular member of staff who has been supportive to you?

> What further support would you like?

You may not feel able to be completely honest in this box if you have feedback that might not be warmly received. However, you can manage this by writing about the areas that you would like more of or by highlighting the positives that you have experienced.

For example, if you have found that feedback has been particularly critical, rather than supportive, something like 'The feedback from my lesson observations has been focused on areas to develop' or 'I have found the feedback that focuses on building on my strengths to be the most effective' could be a way of addressing this area. Appropriate bodies are very good at reading between the lines!

At the midpoint (the end of the first year), there may be a situation where the school or induction tutor is concerned that you are not making satisfactory progress against the Teachers' Standards. This is nothing to panic about at this point. It is tough to hear, but the focus will always be on what support you need. The school and appropriate body will work to support you and will put an action plan in place to ensure that you have the best chance possible of meeting the Teachers' Standards by the end of your induction. At any point in your induction journey, if you are told that you are at risk of not meeting the Teachers' Standards, it does not mean that you have 'failed' that term or your induction as a whole. The recommendation as to whether you have successfully completed induction or not will be made at the end of your induction period and not before.

Another important document that you should be aware of (but hopefully will never need) is the induction appeals procedure (DfE, 2012). This outlines the actions that you can take if you disagree with the outcomes of your induction. Of all the NQTs/ECTs that I have mentored, none have ever failed their induction; however, some were at risk of not meeting the required standards early on in the process – often because they had not shared the difficulties that they were experiencing. It is a rare occurrence, but if you find yourself heading that way, it is important that you know what support is out there for you.

I have mentioned the appropriate body a few times in this chapter; this will be either the local authority or a teaching school hub. Their role is to manage the paperwork and to 'sign off' your induction. However, their other role is to provide you with support. If things do become tough or you feel that you are not receiving the support to which you are entitled, then you can reach out to the named contact, details of whom you should have been given by your induction tutor, for advice and support. An appropriate body is also tasked with monitoring and ensuring that schools are providing effective induction. You may be chosen for a moderation visit, but it will not be to scrutinise you as an ECT; it will be to check that you are receiving your correct entitlement. I was moderated twice during my time as an NQT/ECT mentor, and each time the pressure was on me and the scrutiny was on what I did. The ECT/NQT was only ever involved to ensure that what I had said was accurate and to share their view on how things were going for them.

COACHING MOMENT

▶ Who is your induction tutor?

▶ What do you want to get out of your induction period?

▶ What key skills do you want to develop further?

▶ Who is your named contact at the appropriate body?

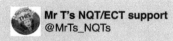 **Mr T's NQT/ECT support**
@MrTs_NQTs

In September, get a meeting booked in with your induction tutor. Make sure you are registered with the appropriate body and that you know who they are (and where you can find a contact number). Plan your targets for the first half-term and make them achievable. #YouGotThis

Getting the most out of your induction

We have been through the process in which you can expect to be involved during your induction. However, there are things that you can do to get the most out of it!

1. **Be open and honest:** If you are finding things hard, reach out and ask for support. Your mentor and induction tutor are there to support you in their roles, and if they know what you need support with, that makes their job much easier; it will also mean that you are less likely to find yourself at the point of feeling unable to cope.

2. **Take ownership of your development:** Alongside the ECF, there will be other aspects of your practice that you want to develop. Seek out the opportunities to work on these (when you feel that you have the capacity) and start to take control of your own development.

3. **Make your targets work for you:** If you know that there are things coming up in the school calendar, or areas that you know you will get the opportunity to address, use these as targets. For example, if parents' evening is approaching, a target linked to communicating with parents can be easily met.

4. **You don't have to complete your induction in one school:** If you secure a post that is fixed-term for one year, or even a maternity contract, any full terms that you complete will count towards your induction. Also, as discussed in Chapter 1, it is very important to find the right school for you. It can be difficult to know what a school is really like until you work in it. If you find that there is a clash of values and things are overwhelming, then you can bank the time already served in your induction period and pick it up in a new school. There is no time scale for completing induction. However, there is a slight caveat: that you can only undertake short-term supply for up to five years before completing induction.

5. **You can work part-time:** Your induction length will be adjusted and can be negotiated with your appropriate body and your school, but you can complete your induction on a part-time basis. If you were to work half of the week, it could take you up to four years to complete induction. However, there is flexibility written into the guidance that the induction period can be adjusted as long as there is sufficient opportunity for an

ECT to be able to demonstrate the Teachers' Standards. The minimum period is one term and could be helpful in cases where ECTs are returning from working overseas or in the independent sector, and have not yet completed statutory induction. It could also be that, as someone working four days a week, you could negotiate to complete your induction within two years providing you have the capacity to be able to demonstrate the standards.

6. **Seize every opportunity:** Observe others, go on learning walks, visit other settings. All these things are great CPD, and non-contact time away from the classroom is an ideal opportunity to engage with this. This time is so valuable, and you will miss it when it is gone!

7. **Don't be afraid to say no:** In your induction, there may be opportunities that come up in which you want to get involved. Equally, there may be those that would cause you more stress than necessary. Don't be afraid to say no. You may feel that it could damage your reputation or limit your professional development somehow, but it is so important to protect yourself and your wellbeing.

8. **Observations are there to help you to develop:** So often we pull out all the stops for an observed lesson that it can be to the detriment of the substance; it also sets a very high bar for yourself and all subsequent observations. As much as possible, do what you normally do, just a bit more polished – that way, the feedback will help you to develop further as a teacher. Remember that the observer wants you to do well; they will look for the positives! If things do go wrong, own it and be reflective. Identify what you would have done differently.

Thoughts from an ECT

You cannot be fully prepared for what you are about to embark on in your first year of teaching. However, I hope that these tips calm your nerves but, most importantly, excite you as you are about to start your challenging, but most importantly rewarding, career in teaching.

After you finish your initial teacher training, you must make sure that you have a relaxing break over the summer. During this period of time, gain access to schemes of work (if you can), curriculum maps and/or the key texts that you might be teaching so that you can be a little prepared for September. Also, if your new school permits you to, go in and meet your department and your new mentor and familiarise yourself with your new environment. It is a lovely way to build relationships with your new department and colleagues.

So, you've had a relaxing, long summer break and it is now September. It is your first INSET day. Be confident and make conversations with colleagues; move into your new classroom, familiarise yourself with school policies and breathe.

Here is the most exciting part – meeting your new pupils! You need to develop your *own* classroom presence, and this comes with time. But the best advice I ever got from my first subject mentor during my ITT year was 'go in tough and then soften up'. You need to set those high expectations to ensure that pupils learn in a safe and effective classroom environment. Then you can get to know your pupils and begin to build that rapport, especially by getting to know pupils' names.

In terms of your ECT framework, every school is different. They decide on their provider and this should be communicated with you. My ECT framework consists of completing an online module each week, which is alongside each half-term so that I have a different strand each half-term. For example: instruction, behaviour, expectations. In addition to the online modules, the expectation is that I get observed every week for approximately 15 minutes by my mentor, with a focus for each observation. Don't be put off by this; it is a fantastic way to continue becoming a reflective practitioner, which is essential as a teacher. You will still have your mentor meetings, which are part of your timetable, as well as your protected time as an ECT. Always *protect* this time. It is vital for you to use it effectively for *your* development as an ECT.

Yes, it is going to be tough getting into a new routine in a new environment, working to adapt SOWs (schemes of work) for your pupils' needs and having that independence in the classroom. But you must make time for yourself and ask yourself, 'Is it urgent?'. If not, then it can wait, because you are the priority. A tired teacher is not an effective teacher.

Overall, you need to find your feet and decide on what works for you as a teacher – every teacher is different and that is the beauty of teaching.

Jamie-Lee Knight, Secondary English ECT

Key takeaways

- The ECF and induction are separate processes.
- You should have access to high-quality CPD, structured around the ECF.
- You should be provided with a named contact at the appropriate body – contact them if you have any concerns about the provision.
- Your induction will be judged against the Teachers' Standards.
- You cannot 'fail' any part of your induction.
- You do not need to collate a folder of evidence.
- Read the statutory guidance document and be aware of the appeals procedure document.

CHAPTER 3
SETTING UP
FOR SEPTEMBER

Mr T's NQT/ECT support
@MrTs_NQTs

About to start your ECT year or move schools at the end of this year? Look at the other classrooms in the school you are going to. This will help you work out things that you MUST have in your classroom and whether you can personalise them or use the school format.

♡   ↻   ♡   ↥

In this chapter we will:

⇒ Consider what needs to be done to prepare your classroom for September.

⇒ Explore potential classroom layouts, making the most of the space that you have.

⇒ Consider what you need to do to make sure that you are prepared for September.

Setting up for September is exciting and nerve-wracking in equal measure. It is important that you create an environment where both you and the pupils feel safe and can thrive. All schools vary as to when you will have access to your classroom. You may have to negotiate with the caretaker when the school will be open and find out when others will be around to answer any specific questions that you may have as you get yourself established. My school was open for the first two weeks and last two weeks of the holiday. I always used the first three days of the holiday to get my classroom organised and sorted. I wanted to know that when I left it was ready for the first day of September!

Prepping the room

You now have a space to make your own: the classroom that will be like your second home during term time and will be the environment that nurtures and supports every learner in your care.

What is important is that it works for you and for them.

First of all, get to grips with what is in there! I inherited my first classroom from a teacher who had been at the school for 11 years. It took me two days just to get to grips with all the 'stuff' that she had left behind. By 'stuff', I mean laminated activity sheets, photocopies, worksheets, activity books, etc.

I made the decision that I would have one cupboard where I would store everything. If I used it, I would then put it back in the other cupboard. (I had heaps of storage in my classroom, but a very strange layout – more about that later.) At the end of the year, anything left in that first cupboard, I chucked. If I hadn't seen the need for it and used it, the chances are that I never would.

Make sure that you take stock of what is in the room. Relabelling drawers with images (see Chapter 8) means that you have to know what is in them, and if you know what is in there, there is more chance that you will use it. If things are labelled, the pupils will also be able to find the resources that they need, and you can grow their independence!

Don't throw out anything that you have inherited straight away, but keep an eye on it. If it doesn't get used in the first year, the chances are that you will never use it.

Once you have established what you have, then comes the task of deciding how your room will look. How will your personality come through? What display spaces do you want? How do you want pupil tables arranged in the room? How will you make sure that children can get around the room safely and are able to access everything that they need?

There are a few basics to keep in mind:

> Have children got somewhere to sit?

> Do they have their own drawer/storage space for snacks or pencil cases?

> Where will they put their coats, lunchboxes and book bags?

> How will they access the regular equipment (pencils, rubbers, pens, paper, etc.)?

> What do you have to have on the walls? What is in the school's policy?

■ Classroom layout

There are huge discussions about classroom layouts and table settings – rows, square table groups, 'U' shapes, 'L' shapes and so on. A lot of the decisions about this may be made for you because of the school's policy or even, potentially, the space that you have available. Consider also how pupils are to be grouped for learning (see the section on flexible grouping in Chapter 8).

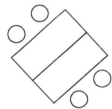

For many years I went with the traditional square shapes, for no other reason than that was the way in which it was done in my school, and for the majority of my experience this is how I had seen tables grouped.

As mentioned earlier, I also had a strange classroom layout. It was a sort of £ shape, with an internal and external door, built-in cupboards and a sink at the back of the room. There was also an excess of display boards –13 in total (although later on I taught in a classroom with 16!).

All of this did restrict me for a while. In my second year, I worked in an Elliott building (one of those lovely pebble-dashed blocks that you see on school grounds). This was a square shape and allowed me a bit more flexibility. I started with squares but quickly moved onto U shapes.

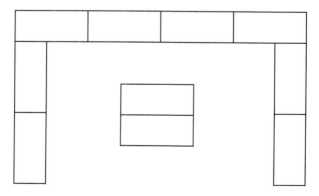

This format allowed me to see all the pupils and move around quite freely to support as and when needed. I also had a flexible table in the middle, where I could group pupils who might need more support in a specific session. I found that this format did limit some of the group dynamics, and pupils were restricted to only speaking to the pupils either side of them. This was great at times, but occasionally stunted the quality of discussion for some pupils. This format worked for me for the two years that I spent in that classroom. I then had to move back into the main building and was once again faced with the prospect of the £ shape.

Now, all this was going on at the time when interactive whiteboards (IWBs) were becoming more commonplace in classrooms, and the expectation was that you had to use the IWB in every lesson. So I now also needed to ensure that all pupils could see the board – not just during carpet sessions but during their working time too. This is when I discovered the 'L' shape. It provided me with the best of both worlds: small enough groups to be able to make the most of the space, but also the ability to organise the room so that all pupils could see the board and still collaborate in groups. It also meant that as a teacher I could get stuck in and support the pupils more effectively.

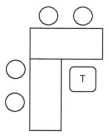

This is the table structure that I have found to be most beneficial to my style of teaching, being able to see all pupils whilst still facilitating group discussion. It is the shape that I have continued to use in my teaching until this day.

'L' shapes can produce strange pathways around the classroom, and this is something else to consider when arranging the furniture. Can the children get from their seat to the resources that they need? Can they get to the fire exit safely? If a child in your class needed to come in on crutches, how easy would it be for them to navigate their way around the space?

When you come to set up your room, you will need to experiment with a layout that works best for you. There may be ideas that you have seen in placement schools that will work in your environment, but they may not. Your classroom environment will evolve over the year – this is absolutely fine. Sometimes we don't know how well something works until we try it! When you have created a layout you are happy with, sit in each seat. What can you see? What will be your path to key places in the room? It can give you a good understanding of how your room will work for your pupils.

COACHING MOMENT

▶ What are your values for the way in which you want children to learn in your classroom?

▶ What can be moved in the room? What is fixed?

▶ What must pupils be able to access with ease?

 **Mr T's NQT/ECT support**
@MrTs_NQTs

When planning your first classroom, you may feel the need to chuck in every idea you have seen during training. Take time to reflect on which ideas align with your core values and the values of your school. Every year there is a system in an ECT class that never gets used!

What's on display?

Every school has its own expectations for displays. They may even have a display policy that will outline what displays you need to have and what those displays should look like. This can be as specific as which colours you can back your board in, to whether work should be single- or double-mounted.

Establishing what is expected is easy if there is a written policy. However, there may not be a written policy but a set of expectations that everyone just knows. Whenever you visit the school, look for what is consistent in every classroom. This will help you to establish what the expectations for your classroom will be. Below, we will explore the most common features that you can expect.

▨ Working walls

Most schools will expect a working wall to capture the learning journey in the key subjects that you are teaching.

In English, most English working walls will include the following:

> an example of the genre that is broken down and analysed to identify its key features

> a space for a vocabulary bank – I always encourage pupils to collect words from their reading and use sticky notes to add to the vocabulary bank (they can be written up larger when checked)

> examples of pupils' work produced during the learning journey – for example, story maps, character descriptions and grammar activities that relate to the topic, such as verbs for writing instructions – or class-generated ideas that can be used as an inspiration bank for their own writing.

All of these elements should be easy to pop up at the end of a lesson, or to photocopy on your way to the toilet or staffroom at lunchtime. Keep your workload in mind when constructing your displays.

In maths, the working wall is likely to show the process and example problems that are being explored that week.

I also used to include practical activities and interactive elements that pupils could engage with or take from when they had completed their work. These ranged from simple fluency activities to problems that would stretch them and allow them opportunities to apply their current learning or revisit previous concepts. All of these were either activities that had previously been photocopied or word problems written on a piece of laminated paper for pupils to engage with – how you will manage the displays is something to be considered in your workload. Make it as non-intrusive as possible.

In other subject areas, these will often follow a similar process: a journey of pupils' learning showing a developing understanding of the concepts being taught.

Working walls are there to capture the learning. They often contain work that has been photocopied straight from children's books or they could be examples that pupils have completed – it is unusual to expect them to be mounted.

■ Celebration

Most schools will want a board where pupils' work can be displayed for celebration purposes. This is likely to be work that is mounted to create a sense of pride in pupils' work. I once set up A3 laminated 'frames' that had each pupil's name underneath, and they could then select their best piece of work that they wanted to put up on display to celebrate. This created a great sense of pride for pupils.

■ Book corner

This will be your opportunity to create a haven for reading. There are so many examples out there on Twitter and Pinterest, but remember that this is your space – make sure that your personality comes through.

The biggest challenge with a book corner is to curate the books within. These questions might help you to make sure that the book corner is as purposeful as it can be.

❭ Can pupils access the books and put them back independently? I remember seeing one classroom where there were so many books that you couldn't pull a book out without bringing three others with it. The easier it is for children to get books out and replace them, the less tidying you will have to do.

❭ Do the books perpetuate stereotypes? Do they reflect the culture of your class? It is so important that pupils see themselves represented in what they read and that they are represented in a positive way.

❭ Were the books written in the last 30 years? Book corners can often be home to the most bizarre books that represented life in the 1960s and lack any relevance for today. If the book is tatty and unappealing to you, the chances are that it won't appeal to pupils either.

❭ How will you arrange the books? By author? By genre? Be clear and label well, so that pupils can maintain the system for you.

❭ How will you encourage pupils to read in the book corner? So often I see immaculate book corners that are immaculate because the pupils never have time to look at them. Plan in purposeful time to use book corners and make the space appealing.

❭ Do you have space to display 'key books'? These can be books that you are reading at the moment, the previous class text or books that complement the topic.

■ Other displays

Some schools may want displays to aid with behaviour management, to share pupil targets or to display the school values, the class charter and so on.

If you are in EYFS, there will be the expectation that 'zones' relating to the areas of learning are created to help children to explore and develop their understanding through continuous provision. Most areas will not change much over the year, but encourage your school to invest in talking tins or postcards, so that you can record additional challenges for pupils to engage with in each area. I used to set challenges for the pupils such as 'What is the tallest building you can create using ten blocks?' in the construction area, or 'Can you find me five of something from around the classroom?' in the maths area.

Your personality

Once you have met the expectations of the school, the rest of the classroom will be yours to put your own spin on. What do you value the most? What do you want to celebrate? What are your interests? You may even be able to create the expected displays in your own style. In the last school at which I taught, the expectation was that you had a working wall for maths and English, but how you made it look was up to you and the children in your class. However, another school I worked in had everything mounted on hessian, and provided headings for each part of the working wall.

Whatever you decide to create, make sure that it has a purpose. So often displays can become wallpaper and lose their power. However, by getting the pupils involved, they can add real purpose to a classroom. Ask them to select the work for the working wall – how would they like to celebrate their success? What interests them? Remember that this is a shared space and, as will be discussed in Chapter 6, using the language of 'our' is so important. Make sure that pupils feel like it is *their* classroom.

COACHING MOMENT

▶ How will you make sure that your personality comes through in your room?

▶ What is important to you when planning your displays? What do you want to celebrate?

▶ How will you make sure that the display areas you set up can be managed and won't create a heavy workload?

▶ How will you keep the pupils involved?

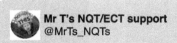 **Daily tip**

Mr T's NQT/ECT support
@MrTs_NQTs

Involve children as much as you can in developing the classroom environment. What works for them? What would be most useful to support them in the classroom? Avoid displays becoming wallpaper if children aren't invested!

♡   ⟲   ♡   ⬆

What do you need to do to be ready?

Being prepared for your first year can be overwhelming and you may never feel fully ready, even when the door opens on the first morning. This is completely normal and it is absolutely OK for you to feel this way. There will be so much that you feel you have to do to be ready, but in this section we will cover the essentials.

▧ Get a big water bottle!

During a busy day in school, finding time to keep hydrated can be tough. A large bottle will help you to keep hydrated; avoid those end-of-the-day headaches and also be a role model to the pupils to show them how important it is to keep drinking.

▧ Plan your lunches

Keeping yourself fed and watered are your main priorities, so making sure that you have something nice to enjoy at lunch is important. In an ideal world you will be able to grab a free school meal at lunchtime, but this may not be an option or available in your school. If you can, prepare meals in the week – the earlier, the better – bulk-cook at the weekend and freeze portions. I have even been known to make my sandwiches for the week on a Sunday night and have them ready for each day. What is important is having nutritious food available to avoid the grab-and-go culture of overprocessed food.

▧ Have some emergency supplies

This will vary from teacher to teacher, but I always used to keep in my bag:

> paracetamol

> ibuprofen

> aftershave/deodorant

> some healthy snacks – fruit bars, oat bars, etc.

> treat snacks – sweets and fun-size chocolate bars for the heavy-marking days/parents' evenings

> a spare tie.

▧ Have a good wardrobe

This means different things to different people and also depends on the subject and age group that you are teaching. Have a few key rules when you are buying or organising your wardrobe.

> What is the school's policy?

- This genuinely varies between schools. Are you allowed to wear open shoes? Can shoulders be exposed? Are smart shorts acceptable in the summer?
- If you have tattoos, does the school expect you to cover them up?

❯ Are the clothes comfortable? This is particularly important for shoes. Make sure that you know your shoes fit and that you can survive a day in them. I always bought shoes from a certain high street retailer. I then tried a different store and the blisters on my feet were the size of golf balls!

❯ Are the clothes professional? My headteacher always used to say, 'If you would wear it to the beach, don't wear it to school.'

❯ What does what you are wearing communicate about you and your personality? Does it say what you want it to?

■ Tidy up your social media

Make sure that your privacy settings are high on all social media channels and change your name if needs be. Parents and pupils will try to find you – make sure that they can't find out your weekend escapades! And when you do post, always consider: 'Would I be happy for this to be on a banner on the school gates?' If the answer is 'no', it's probably best not to post it!

■ Plan in some social events with friends

When you leap on the hamster wheel of teaching, you can lose weeks without having the opportunity to reconnect with your friends and loved ones. Planning things in advance will give them a fighting chance of happening. It may take effort, but maintaining a social connection beyond your school is so important. (More on that in Chapter 4.)

■ Have your QTS certificate handy

You will be emailed a link by the DfE to log in to your teacher self-service portal (https://teacherservices.education.gov.uk/SelfService/Login), where you can access your certificate. This will be important for the school to register you for your induction with the appropriate body.

■ Be prepared to learn a lot and ask lots of questions

Every school is different and will even have its own language (so many schools have different names for the same thing!). I have included a glossary at the end of the book to give you a fighting chance of understanding the array of acronyms that you are likely to encounter, but if you aren't sure, it is important that you ask. Everyone else in the school has been through that learning curve – don't worry about seeking clarification.

■ Don't buy anything

You should not need to buy anything essential for your classroom. However, I always had a slight caveat for books. I used to treat myself to one children's book each month to build my personal library to read with the pupils.

What will your first lesson with the pupils look like?

Some schools may have a clear idea of this already, but others may leave it to you to plan. For me, this first lesson/first day (depending on the age of the pupils you are working with) should always involve:

> Engage with pupils on a personal level – what random fact can you find out about them? With older children, I use Human Bingo: give each pupil a sheet containing statements such as 'Has a younger brother', 'Was born in another country', 'Has an unusual pet' and so on. Pupils then move around the room and find people who meet the criteria and put their name next to the statement. Make sure that you join in too. For younger pupils, circle time to share a favourite hobby, toy or event can be a great way in which to start to build a connection between you and them and between each other.

> Outline expectations (see Chapter 6 for a discussion of this in more depth). Outline what you expect from pupils and what they can expect from you. This could be in the form of a class charter or a verbal discussion, but it is important that these are established – make sure that you reinforce this consistently!

> Start to drip in systems and processes that you want pupils to use throughout the year – for example, should they collect their own resources or will the resources they need always be available on their desks?

> Produce work that can be displayed immediately – it helps to instantly create ownership of the classroom for the pupils.

COACHING MOMENT

▶ Do you know your school's dress code policy?

▶ What social media do you have? Is it for personal or professional use? Would creating a new account help you to manage this distinction?

▶ What is your biggest worry about starting in September? Have you shared this with your colleagues?

▶ What will your first lesson/first day look like?

Thoughts from an ECT

Operation classroom! Having secured a job in a local village school, I remember being so excited to finally have a classroom to call my own and to set up. There was so much to think about, from seating plans to displays, decoration and book corners, and I remember having a thousand and one Pinterest- and Instagram-worthy ideas that I just had to have in my classroom, before I then realised that my tiny village school classroom would allow for maybe three! I viewed my classroom as my second home (in my first two years as a qualified teacher, I think I've spent more time in my classroom than at my new house!), and I knew I wanted it to be calm and relaxing for both the children and myself, but most importantly I wanted to give the children the opportunity to make it their own.

My school had a hessian and black border theme throughout, which suited my neutral classroom idea, and I was also told of some displays that were 'non-negotiables', such as English and maths working walls, vocabulary trees and finally a values display. Having only been given three display boards, I had to get clever, and using black border roll to divide big displays into smaller ones became my go-to. Another problem I had was my inherited trapezium-shaped tables, which could only be placed in hexagonal shapes, which meant either that half the class would have their back to me or that two needed to be joined together to create v shapes, which made getting around the classroom a slalom course. I settled on a mixture of hexagonal and V-shaped tables, but I can confirm that those tables were moved around weekly, if not daily, before I found the right layout that worked for our class – and let me tell you that what worked for them most definitely didn't work for the next class! I also ensured that I had an 'as big as I could possibly make it' book corner (it was still very small) and places for the 'stuff' that manages to just accumulate in a classroom – for example, book bags, umpteen unnamed jumpers, snacks and drinks. Ikea does a wonderful trolley on wheels (RASKOG); I have two: one for snacks and drink bottles and one for me, which follows me around the classroom with pens, stickers, spare equipment and anything else I might need whilst working with the children.

During the summer holidays and my PGCE year, I had prepped a whole array of display items and resources, from birthday displays, noise'o'meters and behaviour charts to end-of-the-day questions, reflection questions and emotion check-ins – the list was endless. I actually only ended up using about three and, looking back, I would prep the necessities and must-haves and then work on an 'as needed' basis. Take the rest of your 'free' time to relax, because once term starts, free time is as hard to come by as a photocopier that doesn't go into meltdown five minutes before a really important lesson observation! For example, my noise'o'meter, with personalised Bitmojis, which took me hours to put together, was never used and fell down a sideboard to be forgotten about until the following summer, when the cupboards got moved for a deep carpet clean! Focus on things that the children will use, that will add meaning to their day and, most importantly, that can be kept up to date pretty quickly. It might not look the most Instagram-worthy display, using hand-written flip charts and sticky notes, but it is quick, easy and, most importantly, relevant and useful for the children.

Top tips for classroom set-up:

1) Have a little area where important reminders, lists, timetables and notes can be pinned and therefore easily found amongst the ever-growing pile of 'really important things I will get done/read/fill out'.

2) When using a staple gun, angle it at a 45° angle so that the staple doesn't lie flat against the display board – it will save you hours when taking displays down!

3) Use handwritten cardboard bunting for display titles. It saves on paper, laminating pouches and your precious free time and it also looks very effective!

4) If you do have to laminate things for displays (they last much longer), use matte pouches, as the glare on normal pouches means that the very important high-frequency word display you've spent hours creating can't be seen by half the class, due to the glare from your fluorescent classroom lights.

5) Don't be afraid to admit that something isn't working and try another way.

Ellie Fisher, Primary ECT

Key takeaways

- Create a classroom that embodies your values for the way in which you want pupils to learn.

- Make the displays in your classroom purposeful and pertinent to you and your learners.

- Being personally prepared for September is important; ensure that you have the systems in place to protect your own wellbeing, and also your privacy when considering social media.

- Your first lesson/day with your pupils should be a chance to get to know them and to establish expectations.

CHAPTER 4
SELF-CARE AND MANAGING WORKLOAD

 **Daily tip**

 **Mr T's NQT/ECT support**
@MrTs_NQTs

It's OK to say no! As an ECT you may feel pressured to say yes to every opportunity. If it will impact on your wellbeing, say no. No one will think less of you. It will allow you to say yes to the opportunities you do feel comfortable with. #YouGotThis

♡   ↻   ♡   ⬆

In this chapter we will:

➡ Identify strategies that you can use to look after yourself both physically and mentally.

➡ Discuss strategies to help you to manage your workload.

➡ Help you with strategies to identify sources of stress and anxiety and explore methods to address these.

Teaching is a career that will take the time that you give to it. It is important that you know how to protect yourself and your physical and mental wellbeing. From my own experience, there have definitely been peaks and troughs throughout an academic year and throughout my career. What I have learned is that it is OK to not be OK, and that some days enough is good enough!

Looking after your physical wellbeing

Teaching is a hugely rewarding job; however, we cannot gloss over the fact that it is a hugely demanding one too, and that it can take its toll on our physical and mental wellbeing. I remember the feeling of exhaustion in my NQT year as I crawled towards the end of my first term. I had no voice, I could not stay awake past 9.00 pm most nights and everything was effortful. I am sure that it was chocolate and caffeine that got me through the last week of term!

Since that first year, I tried ways in which to protect myself and ensure that I could make it to the last week of every term in one piece.

Basic things first:

■ Eat well

Avoid foods that are going to give you a sugar crash in an hour's time. Make sure that you eat proper food and avoid too many processed meals. I am a huge advocate of eating lots of red berries. They give you a natural lift and are packed full of vitamins.

In peak cold season, take vitamin C and zinc tablets to boost your immune system.

■ Drink plenty of water

I once read a statistic that teachers and doctors are most likely to suffer with kidney stones, as they often go long periods without drinking. I have never managed to verify this, but having a decent water bottle on hand to keep you hydrated will avoid that end-of-the-day headache and keep you functioning well.

■ Keep up with engaging in sport and exercise that you enjoy

I know that finding time for this can be a challenge, but I always found that if I spurred myself on to go and play tennis after a busy day, I felt so much better and had more energy the next day. This had a positive impact on my mental health as well.

■ Sleep

I am lucky that rarely have I had a problem sleeping (except for Sunday nights – I don't know many people who sleep well that night). I have found that having a clear bedroom routine helps (I quite like predictability). Having the same pattern and structure for the half-hour before sleep is really beneficial. This can look however you want it to, but try to avoid screen time before bed; if you need to look at a screen, use a blue light filter.

What is important is that you associate your bed with sleep. Avoid lying awake in bed for too long. Reset yourself; get out of bed, read and restart a routine before heading back to bed. Also, keep a notepad next to your bed for those random things for the to-do list; you can park them out of your brain for the night and not have to worry about forgetting them.

■ Look after your voice

For the first four years of my career, I would lose my voice by Christmas. Like any muscle, your vocal cords can become strained, and teaching day in, day out can put a strain on them as your body adjusts to the way you need to project your voice in teaching. Try to use non-verbal cues when you can, and when you need to project, bring your voice from your diaphragm rather than your throat. I made sure that I kept hydrated and, at the first sign of my voice going, I gargled with salt water. I also tried to avoid too much caffeine, as it tightens the vocal cords.

Looking after your mental wellbeing

Lots of things that you do for your physical wellbeing have a positive impact on your mental wellbeing and vice versa. However, there are some specific things that can be particularly helpful to protect your mental health whilst teaching.

■ Find the positives

I think that one of the key personality traits of a teacher can be to see the negatives in situations and to focus on these. However, there will be positive moments each day that can help to keep us buoyant and remind us why we do this job. Sometimes it can be a pupil grasping something with which they have struggled, or a lesson that has gone particularly well. There may even be tangible things that you can keep: an email or letter from a parent, an email from the SLT, a note, picture or card from a pupil. Put these things in a scrap book or a box in your cupboard, so that on the day that things have not gone well at all, you can have a look through and remind yourself that you are absolutely doing your best and #YouGotThis!

■ Say no to things

As an ECT, there can be the self-expectation that you have to say yes to everything that you are asked to do. However, there is no pressure to do this. There may be things that you do feel comfortable doing and that you are able to do within your skillset that won't stress you out. For example, they may ask you to lead an after-school club of your choice – pick something that you enjoy and agree to lead it on a night of the week that won't impact you too much. However, if you are asked to play the piano in assembly next week and the last time you played an instrument was the recorder in Year 4, say no! No one will judge you for saying no. It also gives you capacity to say yes to the things that you will actually enjoy.

■ Be sociable

Teaching can be quite lonely. You spend most of your working day with children and have limited time to interact with other adults. Using breaktimes and lunchtimes to sit with colleagues to talk through the day and to build a personal relationship can make work a much better place to be. Some of the best times that I have had in school have come from laughing with colleagues in the staffroom. In schools, there can often be a 'fun sponge'; this is the person who has a negative view on everything – often the view that if teaching isn't hard and you are having fun, then you aren't doing it right! Steer clear of these people. Find those that energise and inspire you.

■ Be sociable with non-teachers

I have often thought that a collective noun for a group of teachers should be a 'moan'. When teachers meet each other outside of school, the focus can often be on problems and negative experiences in teaching. Having non-teachers to socialise with can help you to have a break and to switch off from teaching for a time, and also help you to step out of the teaching bubble in which we often find ourselves!

■ Talk to people if you are feeling overwhelmed

My pinned tweet since I started my Twitter account has been about reaching out and seeking support. Schools are hugely supportive places and there will be people who will happily help you if they know that you are finding things tough. But you do have to let them know. So often I have had NQTs/ECTs cry on me because things have become overwhelming. Reaching out before this point can make a huge difference and support can be put in place. Sometimes, having that conversation with your colleagues can be tough, and you may be concerned that they will view you in a negative light because of how you are feeling; however, in my experience, schools are hugely supportive places and this honesty will allow your colleagues to be able to offer you the support that you need.

If you feel that you would rather talk to someone removed from the school environment, Education Support offer free confidential support to anyone in education: 08000 562561 or www.educationsupport.org.uk

COACHING MOMENT

▶ What is important for you to make time for in your personal life?

▶ What opportunities do you have to socialise with others? Do you take them?

▶ Who would you feel comfortable and confident talking to if you were starting to feel overwhelmed?

Mr T's NQT/ECT support
@MrTs_NQTs

Take time to monitor your own wellbeing. There will be plenty of additional pulls on your time at key moments of the year. Make sure that you plan in time for you and prioritise your own wellbeing so that you can get to the school holidays in one piece!

Managing your workload

Workload and work–life balance are two of the biggest challenges for teachers and, often, managing these areas is not easy. There can be key times of the year when you are having demands placed on you from different sources – school events, reports, parents' evenings, data drops, pupil progress meetings – all whilst still doing the day-to-day job of ensuring that pupils get the best education possible.

There are some things that you can do to help you to achieve a better work–life balance and to take control of the workload.

Know your productive times

There are times of the day when you will be more productive than others. For me, this was always after school between 4.00 pm and 6.00 pm. In this time, I could always achieve the most, so this was when I tackled my more involved tasks. Some of my colleagues were most productive first thing in the morning. They would be in at 7.30 am to focus on the tasks that needed the greatest focus. This would not have worked for me (I am not a morning person). I could have arrived at 7.30 am, but would then have staggered around like a zombie for 30 minutes – not the best use of my time! Once you have identified these peak times, plan to use your time to the greatest effect. Save the photocopying for a less productive time of the day!

■ Plan your week carefully

Most weeks, you will know when the staff meeting is and when deadlines are for things to be completed. If you are aware of these timings when you are planning lessons (see Chapter 7 for more support with this), devise lessons that are more practical, that can be live-marked or that don't require huge amounts of preparation. It will free up time for you to be engaged with meetings and to complete those other tasks, without fretting about the pile of marking in the classroom.

■ Maximise your PPA time

When I first started teaching, PPA did not exist. I am still not quite sure how I functioned without it! But this has made me incredibly grateful for it, and I make sure that I use it wisely to achieve what I can within the allotted time. Having planned for my own class and worked with a team on planning as part of a three-form-entry school, I have experienced the positives and challenges of both. When planning for my own class, I found that I was less distracted by others and I could focus on what worked for my children. When working as a planning team, the workload could be divided and I wouldn't have to plan everything from scratch – just tweak for my pupils. However, there are challenges to both approaches. Sometimes I struggled for ideas when it was just me, and when planning as a team sometimes we could talk an idea around for an hour and have nothing formalised at all! Whichever situation you find yourself in, it is important that you use the time effectively; sometimes that extra biscuit in the staffroom is necessary, but at times it is important for your own workload to bite the bullet and crack on!

■ Block your time

Teaching, and all the other jobs that go with it, will take as much time as you are willing to give it. Assign a specific amount of time that you are going to work for each day. It may be a number of hours – for example, two hours after school each night – or a deadline, leaving the school at 5.30 pm and not taking anything home. In order to make the most of this time you need to:

Prioritise!

During those less-productive times, I can have a real butterfly brain, flitting from one task to the next without actually completing anything. Prioritising is important to make sure that what absolutely needs to get done gets done.

You may have seen prioritisation matrices that talk about importance and urgency. These do go some way in helping to prioritise but, from my experience, the advice that I always give is to consider, in order of priority:

1. Which task will have the biggest impact on the children's learning?
   - marking, feedback, planning, lesson preparation, seeking advice from the SENDCo about a child in your class
2. Which tasks will help you to feel more in control?
   - getting your data on the system, tidying up your desk, getting organised for next week, printing off next week's spelling lists
3. Which tasks are nice to do but aren't a priority yet?
   - tidying up your displays, laminating resources

Getting the things done that have an impact on children's learning and then using the rest of your time to chip away at some of the other tasks can help you to feel in control and to prioritise where you need to focus your efforts.

■ Control what you can

I have seen colleagues waste huge amounts of time trying to adapt what they are doing when things change. Taking some time to process next steps is important, but often we can spend that time becoming anxious about how we will need to spend even more time changing everything that was planned, which then exacerbates that anxiety and adds to the stress because we don't have any time to action the changes that are needed. You cannot control the fact that the company coming in to do an assembly has cancelled, but you can control how you respond and what you do in those moments. Process the information – curse under your breath if necessary – but then step into action and regain control.

Remember that some days enough is good enough. As teachers, we want to do the best that we can for the pupils we teach, but we also have to be realists. Not every lesson will be outstanding. Not every lesson will have the razzamatazz and 'wow moments' in. This is OK. Teaching is a marathon, not a sprint. You have a year with the pupils you teach to help them to secure their progress. I am not suggesting that you should not be doing the best for the children in your class, but having time to focus on you and not burning out will enable you to be in the class each day, and for some children the consistency of you being there is the best that you can give them. Remember, your individual lessons do not give an accurate reflection of you as a teacher. It is that continual presence, your relationship with pupils and pupil progress over time that truly reflect the quality of you as a teacher.

COACHING MOMENT

▶ When are your most productive times of the day?

▶ How easy do you find it to prioritise the right things?

▶ How do you react when things change? What can you take control of in those moments?

Mr T's NQT/ECT support
@MrTs_NQTs

When you finish on Friday, leave the school bag at work! It will help you switch off. If this feels a bit extreme (and there won't be a potential data breach), leave it in the boot of the car! Make sure it is out of sight, not lurking in the corner of the room staring at you, to help you relax. #YouGotThis

Managing your own emotions

This is something that I have not always found easy. Being able to identify where stress comes from and what triggers this reaction takes time and a sense of self-awareness that I have not always had. There are some obvious sources – Ofsted, *that* parent marching across the playground towards the classroom – but there are other elements that slowly erode your resilience that it is important to recognise.

■ Control what you can

I know that I mentioned this in the previous section, but being able to recognise the fact that you cannot control certain elements and making peace with it saved me so much wasted time and energy. You cannot control the actions of colleagues or parents, but you can control how you respond and the way in which you move forward. You cannot control the Ofsted phone call, but you can ensure that you feel prepared for the lesson that you teach and the knowledge that you have of the children.

Whilst we are on the Ofsted topic, I often get asked what ECTs can expect from an Ofsted visit. They may watch you teach or they may not. It depends upon the size of the school/department and the focus of their visit. But remember, they are not judging you in that moment; they are confirming the judgements and views of the SLT. They will want to speak to you about the support that you are receiving and your access to the ECF. Also be prepared for a question on safeguarding!

■ Find your tribe

I touched on this previously too, but finding those colleagues and people in school who energise you can help you to steer clear of those who drain you. This does not mean creating an echo chamber of everyone who thinks like you – find those with whom you can have a healthy debate and challenge, but also those with whom you can have a laugh and who will fire you up about the day.

■ Set your own deadlines

I love a deadline; it gives me a clear focus and motivation. However, it can also be a source of stress. I will create my own personal deadlines before those that are set by the person who has asked me to complete something. I treat this as my deadline, but I also know that sometimes a safeguarding disclosure can happen at the moment when I had set aside time to tackle the data on the system! Having your own deadline allows time for a bit of flexibility in what you are doing.

■ Try not to overanalyse

This is still one of those pieces of advice that I need to take on board myself. My tendency is to reflect on situations continually. However, I have come to the position that every decision we make is based upon the information that we have at that point in time. It is important not to doubt that. If new information comes to light, we can adjust and we may then reflect on how we would deal with it next time, but don't doubt the decisions that you have made.

■ Swallow the frog!

This is an odd expression but it is about having those tricky conversations. Always seek support from experienced colleagues, but if you know that you need to have a difficult conversation with a parent, go for it! The analogy comes from how the thought of having the conversation, like swallowing a frog, is quite unpleasant. But when you are in the moment, it slides down quite easily and can help you to feel so much better afterwards. Always have a member of the SLT with you or nearby in case you need support in those moments.

■ Take a moment

When you find your anxiety levels rising, stepping away from the situation to regroup, when you are able to, can be important. Find ways in which to refocus your mind. Mindfulness, stilling and focused breathing can all be ways to help you to recentre and regain control. This can also be a great strategy if the to-do list feels overwhelming. Sometimes we feel the need to keep going during the day, but this can be unproductive. Instead, take five minutes to be still (eating a biscuit during this time is optional). A few moments of still and calm can help you to focus on what to do next.

Everybody's triggers and sources of stress will be different. What is key is that as you identify them, you find ways in which to start to take control of them.

COACHING MOMENT

▶ What causes you anxiety/stress at work?

▶ Which of these things can you control?

▶ What strategies do you already have to support you when things become challenging?

Thoughts from an ECT

As an early career teacher, you will be learning to juggle a plethora of responsibilities, which can be a steep learning curve. What I have learned in the past year is that your own health and wellbeing is a responsibility that must remain a priority over all others. This is a foundation to being effective in other areas and must therefore come first. To help you to navigate this, three tips that have helped me have been the Three Bs: boundaries, being honest and being passionate about something for yourself.

Boundaries

The main reason why I became a teacher – to help others – is the reason why I struggled to prioritise my own wellbeing in my first year. I found it difficult to limit the amount of time given to all responsibilities, with my perception that others were relying on me to be perfect. As an ECT, I found myself needing to say yes to everything that I could do to help the class, the school and the parents. My passion to do a good job and prove myself led to my need to always do everything for everyone. But, in doing this, I forgot how to help myself. I fell into the common problem in which ECTs find themselves by staying far later than other colleagues. There will always be a never-ending to-do list of jobs; in this first year, you have to navigate what you *could* and what you *should* do. When I realised this, I gave myself the boundary that I needed to start leaving earlier to adjust my work–life balance. To help to decipher between the 'could' and 'should' jobs, you have to reflect on what the impact of the job will be. To help change my perception that I had to make everything perfect, I gave myself a time by which I had to leave school and started to share my to-do list with my teaching assistant (you can involve anyone you trust). The process of talking through my list and having someone question why I *should/could* do each job helped me to learn to decipher between them independently. Months later, it has become natural to prioritise the jobs I should do, allowing myself to go home and enjoy an evening to rest when there are jobs that I could do. In sharing this, I hope that you can create these boundaries for yourself from the beginning; ask yourself these questions and focus on the jobs that you should do, not could do. If the to-do list only has *could* jobs, then you *should* go home.

Being honest

From personal experience, schools are very supportive environments, with an eco-system of people that will be able to offer guidance or support. There is one key hurdle to getting this support and guidance, and that is that you have to be honest with colleagues, with mentors and with yourself. The people around you cannot offer help if they do not know a) that you need it and b) what you need help with. I almost found myself forgetting that every experienced teacher I was looking to for advice started out exactly like me. Talking about my practice more allowed me to reflect and improve; the opportunity to do this shouldn't only be seen as a scheduled conversation with your mentor. A great space I found to do this in was the staffroom at lunch. If I felt that a lesson hadn't gone how I thought it would or I had a specific behaviour issue, colleagues could talk this through with me in five minutes. They offered examples of when they had experienced this before, sometimes offering examples with the same child taught previously, and strategies that had worked for them. Sometimes they recognised that ECTs can just be hard on themselves and offered reassurance that I would be doing a good job. Develop these relationships with your colleagues to have these honest conversations, and you will benefit from them; just don't be afraid to ask for advice.

Be passionate about something for yourself

Your ECT time has the potential to take over your life if you don't set boundaries. To make sure that you are preserving your own health, find one thing that you do for yourself every week. It sounds simple yet changed my experience when I implemented this regularly. I found that having a routine helped me to stick to this, but the important part of it is that the activity is something that you enjoy. For myself, I started swimming on the same day after a staff meeting. This time needs to give you the opportunity to turn off from work and enjoy something about which you are passionate. It can be anything, but it needs to be protected time for yourself.

Hannah Gatfield, Primary ECT

Key takeaways

- Protecting your physical and mental health is important. Don't neglect these areas.

- Finding ways in which to take control of your workload is important; try to be proactive and not reactive.

- Control what you can. Acknowledge the frustration but move forward with what you can take charge of.

- Identifying sources of stress and anxiety is important. Develop strategies to deal with them as you identify them, and reach out for support.

CHAPTER 5

IT TAKES A
VILLAGE

 **Daily tip**

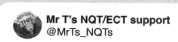 **Mr T's NQT/ECT support**
@MrTs_NQTs

Build a positive relationship with your TA quickly; they will be an invaluable source of advice and support, and also the person most likely to bring you a hot drink if you don't make it to the staffroom! Make time to talk about the children in your class, as well as just 'chat' about the random things in life.

♡   ⟲   ♡   ⬆

In this chapter we will:

➡ Identify the importance of working with colleagues in order to support pupil outcomes.

➡ Explore ways in which to maximise your relationship with your teaching assistant/support staff.

➡ Understand the role that external partners can play in supporting pupil outcomes.

This chapter is about how you can create positive relationships with your colleagues in school and beyond, to be able to achieve the best outcome for pupils.

The chapter is named after the famous saying that 'it takes a village to raise a child'. This is absolutely key to your practice. Yes, you have a responsibility for the pupils in your care and their achievements, but the maximum that you will see them for is around 27 hours a week in primary school and ten hours a week in secondary school (if you teach them a core subject and they are in your form). Utilising the expertise of other colleagues and services will be integral to you maximising this time with pupils, and by developing effective working relationships with your TA, you can work collaboratively to provide the best opportunities outside of the time that you have with them.

Expert colleagues

You will have many experts in your school, and seeking their advice and wisdom is such a key part of your development and will allow you to get the best outcomes for the pupils in your care. In this section, we will identify some of the key staff to know and draw upon and how best to implement their advice.

Special educational needs and disability coordinator (SENDCo)

The SENDCo is a pivotal role in school, and whoever this person is will be an advocate for achieving the best outcomes for all pupils in the school, but specifically those on the special educational needs and disability (SEND) register. In an ideal world they would have little to no teaching responsibility and would be able to spend time supporting teachers and working with pupils on the SEND register. This might happen in a secondary or large primary school, but in a smaller school they are likely to have at least a part-time if not full-time teaching responsibility, or may even be the headteacher. They will be able to support you by observing pupils and being a 'more knowledgeable other' and a sounding board with whom to share your concerns. They will ask you about what the child can do and what their strengths are, and then will support you in how to use these to develop the areas of need. They will take the lead in any paperwork that needs compiling and will support you in review meetings for those pupils on the SEND register or for education, health and care plan (EHCP) annual reviews. They will also monitor and support with provision mapping for the pupils in your class and will ensure that you are developing your quality-first teaching (see Chapter 8), as well as supporting with specific provision for pupils with SEND.

They may want to observe the pupils in your classroom in order to support you. They may also identify specific interventions for the pupils in your class, ensuring that any specialist provision is sought and implemented.

Designated safeguarding lead (DSL)

The role of the DSL is to coordinate and lead the safeguarding provision in the school. You will receive safeguarding training in your school from the DSL to explain the school's specific systems and procedures. The DSL will be the person who collates safeguarding information and actions any disclosures that need escalating to the local safeguarding children board (LSCB) or social services. However, one of their key identified roles is that of advice and support. If you have any concerns about a child's welfare or if a parent has disclosed that they are struggling and need support, the DSL will be able to signpost support for the parent and support you with your next steps in supporting that child. At times, you may not see any 'action' being taken, but things will be happening in the background and a wider picture being compiled to make sure that the action taken is the right one for the pupil and all those concerned. If you ever have any immediate concerns or if you have had a distressing disclosure made to you, the DSL is your first port of call; they will reassure and support you.

Curriculum leads

If there is a particular subject or area that you are finding challenging, or one that you are looking to explore in more depth, the curriculum or subject leads can be a great resource to tap into. They will have a deeper knowledge of their curriculum area and have a full overview of how what you are teaching fits into the bigger picture. Seek opportunities to observe them teaching their subject and have them observe you. Even better, ask them to undertake a joint observation with you of another colleague, so that they can talk you through the pedagogical approaches being used and help you to identify the impact on the pupils. The impact that this can have on your professional development is incredible.

Support staff

The school secretary, the cook, the caretaker, lunchtime supervisors, technicians and librarians are all experts in their field and can make a huge difference to your ECT year. Take them a cuppa, make time to speak to them and ask them how their day is going – not to always get something back but to be a good colleague to work with. You may need to draw on these relationships at different points throughout your year, to support you and the pupils.

> The secretary is your first line of defence against parents and often the keeper of the key to the stationery store. Be nice to them; take time to speak to them and find out about them. Just by building a relationship with my school secretary, I used to get notes saying 'I've had Mrs X on the phone but I have told her that you aren't free to speak to her until after school'. Other colleagues had a phone call to their rooms saying 'Mrs Y is on the line and she's not happy!'. Also, I never ran out of glue sticks in my classroom! ☺

> The cook – hopefully this is an obvious one. The day you forget your lunch or you planned to do an investigation and have run out of flour, they will be your saviour!

> The caretaker keeps the school going and makes sure that you can do your job safely. Having that positive relationship means that when you need a shelf putting up, you won't have to wait very long.

> Lunchtime supervisors truly have the most challenging job in the school; they come in for an hour in the middle of the day, when there is no structure and the ratio is one adult to what feels like a million pupils, and get paid very little for doing it. Yet they turn up each day, and a great lunchtime supervisor is worth their weight in gold, as they will try to solve issues for you so that you can teach in the afternoon. Make sure that your kids are ready on time and that you pick them up on time at the end of lunch.

> Technicians and librarians also play a huge part in the life of the school, ensuring that you are prepped to teach.

COACHING MOMENT

▶ Do you know who the DSL and SENDCo are?

▶ Are the pupils who may need more support on your radar?

▶ Which curriculum areas do you have an interest in or wish to develop further?

Mr T's NQT/ECT support
@MrTs_NQTs

Daily tip

When you get the opportunity to visit your new school, use the time to get to know the staff in the school: the school secretary, caretaker, cook and cleaner. These are the people who can make a huge difference to the smooth running of your ECT years!

Working with a teaching assistant (TA)

Having another adult in the room that is experiencing the class in the same way as you can be hugely bonding and lead to a rewarding relationship.

However, these relationships do not always come naturally and can take work to get right. As an ECT, the chances are that you will be supported by a TA who has been at the school for a long time. In my case, I was working with a TA who had been at the school longer than I had been alive! This can be hugely intimidating, and I often found myself questioning everything I did and wondering constantly whether I was being judged. However, as time went on and our relationship grew, we developed a really effective relationship that supported the pupils' holistic achievement.

When you first meet your TA, don't get down to business straight away. Find out about them as a person and build a personal connection that will help to strengthen your professional one. A cup of tea and a slice of cake can help speed this along!

Once you know them as a person, it is then about identifying their strengths, what they feel passionate about and confident with, and how these can be best used in the classroom.

Over my career, I have worked with a range of TAs, some who have been very happy to teach the whole class, some who have had strengths in maths and some who have had strengths in creating displays. All of them wanted to be able to give the children the best opportunities possible.

Knowing and utilising your TA's skills and interests is so important to achieving a positive working relationship.

Here are a few ways in which you could consider utilising your TA in your lessons:

> Working with a focus group of pupils: If there is a specific concept with which a group of pupils is struggling or needs further challenge, utilising your TA to work with that group can be beneficial. A word of caution – this should not always be pupils with SEND or previously lower-attaining pupils. These pupils often have the most complex needs, so should be supported by the most qualified person in the room (that's you).

> 'Helicoptering' and triaging the students whilst you support a focus group: Utilising your TA to 'live mark' and assess pupils as they are circulating around the room can give you time to provide a focused input with a group of pupils. By checking in regularly with your TA, you can also get a sense of how the class is doing and can also regroup pupils if there are some key misconceptions being identified.

> Delivering specific interventions: There may be some pupils who need support beyond your quality-first teaching and require specific interventions. The timing of these is always challenging; with over 20 years' experience, I still haven't found the answer to this! However, we also need to be mindful that some students may not be benefitting from an input around the use of relative clauses if English is not their first language and they have

only been in the country for four weeks. This would be a prime time for your TA to be supporting with basic vocabulary so that the pupils are able to interact socially and to make their needs known effectively. On the other end of the scale, it may be that there are pupils who are confident with the content being discussed, with the benefit for them coming through focused intervention work on how to apply their knowledge in different situations. Additionally, there may be specific interventions that have been directed by an external agency, such as precision teaching (https://develop.clf.uk/content/pedagogy/precision-teaching-an-introduction/), that need to be completed.

> Pre-teaching or catch-up teaching: Both of these techniques will depend on your knowledge and assessment of the pupils. Pre-teaching can be great for pupils who are struggling with language comprehension. If you know that there will be technical vocabulary used in your session, by asking your TA to go through this language before the lesson starts or when pupils first arrive in school, and to explain it with the use of visuals and a clear context, this can avoid the pupil sitting through an explanation without knowing what you are talking about. Post-lesson it may be that there are a few pupils who need more support to secure the concept. Utilise your TA and provide time for this in other parts of the day or even at the start of the next session, to ensure that pupils are ready for the next concept.

Some of the strategies for deploying your TA may be happening whilst you are delivering the main input at the start of the lesson. This is a crucial point and it is important that you are clear about what you want your TA to be doing during this time. It can often be a wasted time for them, and I frequently see TAs just sitting and listening to the input, rather than having a clear direction. If you need your TA to be engaged in your teacher input, here are some approaches that you might find useful to maximise their presence and support:

> Observing pupils: They can use sticky notes to jot down who is/is not engaging and who is/is not contributing – such as that one pupil who never seems to know what they are doing when you set them to their task!

> Acting as a scribe: Sometimes, when you want to gather ideas from pupils quickly, having your TA scribe can be hugely beneficial – particularly for a session where you may be collating a vocabulary list – and it can maintain the flow of the lesson much more effectively.

> Supporting with behaviour management: Carefully positioning your TA near to some of your more 'challenging' pupils can make your input run a lot more smoothly. By the same token, ask your TA to spot those pupils who have been listening well and demonstrating your expectations so that they can be publicly praised. This raises their profile with the pupils, reinforces expectations and improves behaviour too.

> Getting into role: Sometimes I have used my TA to create what could be defined as a 'skit'. Involving them in demonstrating a concept or discussing with them beforehand how you want them to respond to a certain situation or question can be useful, either for you both to role-model expected behaviours or to use as a teaching point to address misconceptions. I have done this to demonstrate listening skills, where the TA talked to me whilst I modelled bad listening habits for the pupils to identify. (Make sure that your TA is comfortable with this!)

Whatever strategies you are using to deploy your TA, it is important that these are communicated effectively. Time is the most valuable commodity in schools, and time to talk to your TA is often hard to come by. In my experience, TAs are often not paid to come in until the school day starts, and many will also be lunchtime supervisors. Finding time in between to communicate clearly and effectively is challenging. You may have a TA who works the whole day but who is willing to stay after school or arrive early to ensure that they are prepped for the day ahead. However, even if they are willing to do this, please remember that they are not paid a 'salary'. Don't continually expect them to do things beyond their contracted time.

The effective use of a TA has been the focus of plenty of research. I have found the Education Endowment Foundation guidance (EEF, 2018) particularly useful and workable when considering my own practice.

So, how can we communicate effectively?

If you can, agree an assembly time once a week where you can meet to give an overview of the week ahead and to talk about key focus pupils.

Make sure that your TA is included in the planning. Make their role clear and guide them in how you want them to support the learning. For example, providing question prompts for them to use with the pupils can be really beneficial.

Give them the planning in a timely manner and make sure that you give them the opportunity to ask any questions.

Agree a system for feedback. If your TA has to rush off at the end of the morning session to do lunchtime supervision, create a system (sticky notes often work well) where they can let you know how the pupils got on. The system that my TA and I eventually settled on was that she would put away the books of the pupils who were secure and leave out the books of those pupils who may need more support. She had written notes on their books or on sticky notes to let me know where they may need more support. This then meant that I could look through their books and decide on next steps for those pupils.

Other systems that I have trialled with varying success include:

> A specific feedback sheet with a clear structure:

		Mon	Tue	Wed	Thu	Fri
Maths	Pupils exceeding					
	Pupils who need more support					
	Comments					

This gave me a quick overview and was not time-consuming for the TA. Each day, they would write names in the first two boxes and then any general comments about the activity in the final box.

> Annotating the planning: Providing the TA with a copy of the planning for them to annotate and leave in a folder in the classroom, so that I could then review their notes at the end of the morning session or at the end of the day.

The most important thing to remember when working with your TA is that you are both in it together and working for the best outcomes for the pupils. Your TA has the pupils' best interests at heart, and sometimes this can lead to a 'clash of personalities'. As a teacher, you have ultimate responsibility and accountability in your classroom. Your TA should be under your direction at all times, and you should be confident that you know what they are doing and how it is going.

Being a teacher means that you also have to manage the relationship with your TA. If you find that they are not always following your instructions or they are not supporting children in the way in which you would like them to, there are a few simple things that can help.

> Go back to basics: Chat to them over a cuppa about how things are going. Are you providing them with enough information? Do they feel clear about what you are expecting of them? Do they feel confident in how you are asking them to support?

> Get them on side: Invite them to share their thoughts and experience with you. Try: 'I am going to try this activity with the pupils today and I would really value your perspective about how you think it works' or 'I am finding that these pupils are not always responding well to the tasks that I am asking them to do, so is there something different that you think I could try?' Never underestimate your TA's viewpoint of the room and their knowledge and experience.

> Be honest: If something isn't working, view it from the perspective that there is more that you could have done – for example, 'I have noticed that you don't always seem entirely sure when working with the pupils, so what else could I do to be able to support you?'

COACHING MOMENT

- ▶ What do you know about your TA beyond the classroom?
- ▶ What are your TA's strengths and skills?
- ▶ How and when do you communicate with your TA? Is this effective?
- ▶ What strategies for deploying your TA are having the biggest impact on pupils' progress?
- ▶ What will your TA be doing whilst you are delivering the key input for the session?

Mr T's NQT/ECT support
@MrTs_NQTs

Daily tip

When you've developed a rapport with your TA, ask 'What went well today?' It starts a positive dialogue. If you feel confident, then ask 'What did I do well today?' or 'Is there one thing I did that could have been better?' TAs can be a great source of feedback for you.

External agencies

There are many external agencies that you may have to work with or need to call upon during your teaching career. We will outline a few here and how they might be able to support you.

■ Speech and language therapist (SaLT)

I have started here because so many pupils now arrive in school with communication or speech difficulties that you will most likely have met a SaLT early on in your career. Their role is to support pupils' understanding and use of language, as well as supporting with the mechanical pronunciation of sounds (although an intense focus on phonics in the Early Years has reduced the need for the latter). Some schools will employ their own SaLT or buy into a SaLT service rather than relying on what the NHS can offer, as waiting times can be excessive for referrals. A SaLT will work with pupils to assess their current level of language and then plan a support package that you/your TA/

a member of the school team/parents will support with delivering to pupils. The programmes of support are normally reviewed every six weeks.

■ Educational psychologist (ed psych)

The role of the ed psych is to assess pupils and identify areas of strength and need. They can support the application for an education, health and care plan (EHCP) and support you as a class teacher in unpicking that pupil you just can't seem to work out! An educational psychologist's time is bought in by the school and it is not cheap, so schools will often prioritise those pupils who are at greatest need. The ed psych will often want to speak to you about the pupil – be prepared to provide the pupil's strengths and areas of need and to discuss the strategies that you have employed already. They will usually observe the pupil in situ in the class, as there may be some aspects of your practice on which they can advise to help you to get the most out of the pupil. They may also work one-to-one with a pupil to carry out a specific assessment that can help to inform targets or provide evidence for an EHCP. They will rarely 'diagnose' a specific learning difficulty but may refer the parents or carers to their GP to support with this if needed.

The first time that you meet an ed psych may be at an annual review of provision. In these meetings, the EHCP will be reviewed, targets will be revised (if necessary) and an understanding of whether the provision has been effective will be discussed. Your SENDCo will help you to prepare for this meeting, but it will be about sharing what has and hasn't worked and your understanding of the pupil's progress against their targets. Be honest: celebrate what is working, but also be prepared to share where further support may be needed. (Make sure that you know and understand the EHCP before this meeting.)

■ Advisory Teaching Service (ATS)

The Advisory Teaching Service (ATS) provides specific support for pupils and will often become involved as a result of a GP, paediatric or educational psychologist referral. Similar to an educational psychologist, their services can be bought in by a school and will often be to support specific pupils. Unlike an ed psych, they have a particular area of specialism. These tend to relate to the four areas of need identified in the SEND Code of Practice (DfE and DHSC, 2015): cognition and learning – pupils who struggle with processing or storing information; communication and interaction – pupils who struggle to communicate effectively or who are unable to interpret and understand people and the world around them; physical and sensory impairment – supporting pupils with a sensory need, e.g. hearing or sight impairments or a physical disability; and social, emotional and mental health – support for those pupils who struggle to process and understand their emotions and may find it difficult to form positive relationships with others, or who are in poor mental health at that time.

The ATS may be involved if a pupil has a formal diagnosis of a specific learning difficulty, or as part of support for an EHCP. They will maintain regular contact with the parents and the school in order to support the pupil both in school and at home.

Child and Adolescent Mental Health Services (CAMHS) or Children and Young People's Mental Health Services (CYPMHS)

This is an NHS agency that may be in contact with the school but will often work with a pupil outside of their setting. They usually become involved through a referral from a GP, but they can be referred by a parent or a school and, if old enough, a pupil can refer themselves. CAMHS will provide support to pupils who may be struggling with their mental health and wellbeing. As a class teacher, you may be asked for information about a pupil's behaviour in school in order to support with a diagnosis or to identify specific strategies that are needed.

■ The Virtual School

The Virtual School is not an actual school, but an organisation that ensures continuity of support and provision for those pupils currently in the care system or who are in the process of being adopted. They will support pupils who have arrived in the school due to being rehomed, or who have been taken into the care system. They will offer additional support and will ensure that the targets and needs of the pupils are being met regardless of the setting. They will liaise between school, home and social services to ensure a coordinated approach. As a class teacher, you may be invited to meetings and asked to share data and information with the Virtual School so that they can monitor progress and provide support for pupils.

Whenever you get to work with expert colleagues within – or external to – the school, there are some key things that you can do to maximise the impact on your practice.

❯ Always arrive with a notebook or a way of capturing what they say – many externals will follow up in an email, but it is never in the same detail.

❯ Make a list of questions before you attend – often externals see a snapshot or may have a focus in their mind before they arrive. Having a clear sense of what you want to get out of the meeting can be useful.

❯ Act on the advice – hopefully this is an obvious one, but it can be frustrating when advice has been given and you can see that it hasn't happened (for whatever reason). Remember that these are experts in their field and they want you and the pupils to be successful.

> If it's not working, or you are unsure, reach out sooner rather than later. External agencies can often only visit once per term or half-term at most, so waiting for the next meeting may be too long, particularly for supporting a struggling pupil or developing your own practice. By being proactive, you are giving yourself and the pupils the best chance at success.

> Be open and honest – whoever you are speaking to will have your or the pupil's best interests at heart. Being honest about your struggles will give you the best chance to move forward and improve the outcomes for all concerned.

COACHING MOMENT

▶ Which pupils in your class have support from external agencies?

▶ Which external agencies already have a presence in your school?

▶ Which external agencies might you be expected to work with over the coming academic year?

Thoughts from an ECT

The title of the chapter 'It takes a village' absolutely resonates with me, as it really does take a whole community to teach. The relationships that you will form with the adults in your school and outside agencies will be crucial to your ECT journey.

As an ECT, I have relied on the adults within my classroom for support, guidance, ideas and knowledge from previous classes they have worked in. This could be how to conduct successful interventions, behaviour management and, of course, those questions from children that you had not anticipated being asked and that moment in which you simply cannot think of how to approach an answer. To give a simple look to your colleague to come and help you out will never be undervalued.

I work in a two-form-entry school, so I have a year group partner who has been such a support to me through this year. I really do believe that you are still learning throughout your whole teaching career, and your ECT years can mould you into the teacher you see yourself being. I have been fortunate enough to learn from a talented teacher, who is patient and supportive. I have shared ideas and asked for help and support in all areas – for example, behaviour management, planning, and data and marking. My favourite sentence, and I have no doubt it is my year group partner's too, is 'Sorry, just a quick question'. The relationship that we have built is so important as it is great to work as a class, but to work as a year group is not only fundamental for learning but also allows the children to be part of a big team, which is fantastic.

Next, I would like to talk about the headteacher, who is such an important part of your journey. They are the decision-makers of the curriculum and decide how you will need to run the classroom, according to the school's road map. My headteacher has very much an open-door policy; this means being able to drop in at a moment's notice for advice or a general chat. Having support with how to move children forward with their learning and being able to discuss any issues, like if you are feeling a little bit behind on work or are struggling with a list that appears to be getting longer rather than shorter, is very beneficial. They have been there – they know how you are feeling and often how best to support you.

The final adults I would like to discuss are outside agencies. In my setting, I have communication with speech and language therapists who are also attached to a family centre. Working effectively with these agencies will really support you with not only knowing the children's families but also supporting the children in class; the professionals have often shared their expertise and resources to enable a successful learning environment. I felt that the support from outside agencies gave me the confidence to continue working towards the same goal.

I do understand that the positive experiences I have had aren't going to be like that for everyone. I would always suggest being patient and always having an open and honest line of communication, surrounded by mutual respect – remember that everyone's aim is to ensure that the children have the most amazing, impactful learning experiences during the year. Teaching is a difficult yet important profession. However, with the support of a village of experts, you will continue to learn and grow and take on a wealth of information to support you on your journey.

Leila Dahou, Primary ECT

Key takeaways

- Seeking advice and support from expert colleagues is an important part of your role.

- Your TA is your most valuable teaching resource; invest in them both personally and professionally.

- Knowing your TA's strengths, skills and passions will support you in deploying them effectively.

- Acting on advice and seeking clarification is beneficial to get the most out of the advice.

- Be open and honest when sharing your strengths and areas of need.

- Working with other agencies can bring in expertise to support the outcomes for pupils.

- Involvement of an external agency may not always lead to a specific diagnosis but it will identify key strategies.

CHAPTER 6
ESTABLISHING EXPECTATIONS

 **Daily tip**

Mr T's NQT/ECT support
@MrTs_NQTs

Your expectations for your pupils will be your own. As long as they're behaviours you're happy with and they create a positive learning environment, don't change them to match others. I like a buzzy classroom, some of my colleagues like it almost silent. Both are productive.

In this chapter we will:

➡ Explore how the way in which we behave impacts on behaviour management.

➡ Identify the importance of building positive relationships with pupils.

➡ Discuss how to establish clear routines and expectations for behaviour.

➡ Identify strategies for how to manage behaviour incidents when they occur.

This chapter will focus on how you can manage the behaviour of the pupils as effectively as possible and create positive behaviour for learning. Please keep in mind that whole books are dedicated to this subject, so this chapter is not going to be a silver bullet to help you to correct every possible behaviour scenario. What it will do is help you reflect on situations and provide you with the confidence to create clear expectations and routines. This will give you the best chance of creating an environment where pupils are clear about those expectations and will want to meet them. When we consider behaviour management, we need to view it from three angles:

> the relationships that we have with pupils and with their peers

> what we can do to prevent issues with behaviour

> how we can deal with the undesired behaviour when it arrives.

Relationships

When thinking about behaviour management, it is often one of those areas of teaching that we feel is 'of the moment'. It feels hard to prepare for beforehand because we are waiting for the reaction of our audience to know how to adapt and move forward.

However, there are a few things that can really help you and that you can plan and prepare for before you even meet your class.

■ Knowing yourself

Teacher presence is one of those things that people feel they either have or they don't have. We all know that person who can walk into a party and command the attention of a room full of people with their latest escapades, and then there are others who are quite happy to sit to the side engaged in meaningful one-to-one conversations. (I am definitely the latter of these people.) Both of these types of people (and the spectrum in between) have what it takes to be an effective classroom teacher. The presence that the first example has can be developed by the second.

I had to develop my teacher persona. Andy is a unassuming chap who enjoys a quiet conversation at the side of the room. Mr T, however, walks into the classroom ready to command the room and is confident standing in front of the pupils, ready to teach them.

To achieve this level of confidence, we need to consider two things: where does the confidence come from and how can we show it?

Confidence develops over time, by recognising how positively presenting as confident is received by the pupils and through seeing the impact that it has on the classroom and pupil behaviour. It is one of those 'fake it until you make it' moments. 'Faking it' it starts with a few simple things.

Teacher persona

Be the character that you want to be. Create your own teacher persona. How does Mr, Mrs, Miss, Ms, Mx behave in the classroom? How do you want the pupils to describe your teacher persona? How can you make sure that this is what the pupils actually think? When you are in your 'school uniform', this can be when you step into that character.

Body language

There are countless pieces of research about how your body language can shape the way in which you are perceived. There is a great TED Talk by Amy Cuddy (2012) that discusses this brilliantly.

When thinking about body language, we think about:

> The way in which we stand: Feet planted on the floor, shoulder-width apart, keeping your back straight and your head up.

> Eye contact: Make eye contact with the pupils as much as you can – don't stare them out as they walk into the room, but make purposeful eye contact when you greet them to acknowledge that you feel comfortable and confident in the room. (Be mindful that some pupils with SEND may not be able to reciprocate – do not force them to.)

> Hands: This is always an interesting one. Some people (like me) talk with their hands. However, too much fiddling can convey a sense of uncertainty. Don't fold your arms – that conveys being defensive and closes you off to the pupils. Try to keep your hands as still as you can, but when you are moving them, keep your palms in an upwards position to show that you are open to the pupils.

> Voice: It is not always what we say but how we say it. Try to avoid too many 'umms' and 'errs'. Also, if you know that there is a word that creeps into every sentence when you are nervous (often 'like' or 'OK'), try to become aware of this so that you can spot it and try to minimise it. I know that this is tough, but it is so important to support the confidence and clarity of what you say. Keep the register of your voice low and clear. When we get overwhelmed, we move into our 'head voice' and the pitch goes up – this shows panic (only dogs and dolphins can hear you) and can weaken the effectiveness of your voice at being able to fill the space.

All of these elements can be practised before entering the classroom and will allow you to walk in with confidence. Practise them in front of a mirror or with willing friends and family.

Knowing your stuff

Being confident in what we teach also manifests itself in the way in which we present ourselves. Think about a subject area in which you feel confident – imagine that you were asked to talk about it for two minutes with no preparation. How would you feel? Now imagine the opposite. You have to talk for two minutes about a subject about which you know almost nothing but you have time to prepare – how does that make you feel?

Being as prepared as you can before stepping into the room gives you the best chance possible to present yourself in a calm and confident way.

COACHING MOMENT

- ▶ How confident do you feel when entering the classroom?
- ▶ Which of the areas of the teacher persona discussed previously do you think would make the biggest impact on how you present yourself?

Presenting as confident

Why is presenting as confident important? Let's think of an example. You are heading to the dentist with toothache. You walk in and the dentist welcomes you with a warm smile, asks about you and speaks with authority about what needs to happen next. Now imagine an alternative scenario: you walk in and the dentist is looking at the floor and shuffling their feet. They ask you to sit in the chair and then start picking up different 'tools' and inspecting them as if they are not sure which to use. How would you respond in these two situations? The first would put you at ease and make you feel relaxed. The second would kick in that fight-or-flight mode; you may squirm around, question everything they do and may even run out of the room!

Pupils are the same; if they don't sense a level of confidence and authority from you, they are more likely to act out to check your boundaries and make sure that you actually know what you are doing. Avoid this by showing them that you belong in the room, through the way in which you present yourself and the way in which you interact with them.

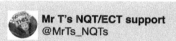 

Mr T's NQT/ECT support
@MrTs_NQTs

When developing your teacher presence, think about your posture. Make sure you stand up straight and hold yourself with confidence. This is also true when meeting with parents. If you look confident, they will have confidence in you.

■ Building relationships

For me, building relationships is key. Knowing your pupils and allowing them to get to know you can be the greatest behaviour management skill that you ever learn.

My own experience has taught me the importance of this. Four years into my teaching career, I experienced *that class* – the one that can make or break you! I am eternally grateful for what they taught me, but it was not a pleasant learning experience. They were fractious with each other, they struggled to build effective friendships and they constantly challenged and questioned me. The first term of the year was 80 per cent behaviour management and 20 per cent teaching. It was tough. By the afternoons I was exhausted, after keeping them on track in the morning. I couldn't give them an inch – they would take the whole metre stick, snap it in half and hand it back! I burned my way through so many different behaviour management strategies to keep some sort of order (I will share some of the most effective ones with you later on in this chapter), with occasional, short-lived success. I was studying for a Masters in inclusive education at the time, and they became the focus of my research.

I spent hours reading and exploring behaviour management techniques, researching theories and ideas to help me make sense of the class and to keep my resilience and positivity at the forefront. Eventually, two theorists became my allies! Bandura's *Social Learning Theory* (1977) and Glasser's 'choice theory' (1997) were the theories. 'Social learning theory' made me realise that I was not offering up enough role models to the pupils. They were seeing behaviour each day that would not build into positive interactions (I spent a lot of time nagging them). However, it was 'choice theory' that really hooked me in. It advocates the idea that all behaviour is a choice and driven by five needs: survival, belonging, freedom, fun and power. This gave me a way of looking at the behaviour of the pupils. But what was more significant to me was that it identifies the fact that the only behaviour that we can truly control is our own. Every individual controls their own behaviour and it is a 'choice' that has consequences. This for me was not a way of absolving myself from managing the pupils' behaviour but helped me to focus the way in which I continued to work with them. I needed to create an environment where the pupils wanted to behave and to make the right choices about their behaviour.

Glasser (1997) advocates seven deadly and seven caring habits:

Deadly habits	Positive habits
Criticising	Supporting
Blaming	Encouraging
Complaining	Listening
Nagging	Accepting
Threatening	Trusting
Punishing	Respecting
Bribing or rewarding to control	Negotiating difference

With this class, I was ticking so many of the deadly habits that I knew I needed to shift to the caring habits!

I started with building relationships. If I wanted the pupils to behave, I would need to make sure that they wanted to. There were a few simple things that I did to try to embody those caring habits:

1. I greeted them every morning at the door with a smile and a welcome, to show that, whatever had gone before, today was a fresh start.
2. During playtimes and at quieter times, I spent time talking to them, showing an interest in their interests and remembering what they had told me so that I could ask about it at another time.

3. When behaviour incidents occurred, I made sure that I spoke about the behaviour, and not about the pupil – for example, 'Pushing your friend Sam is not acceptable behaviour; you are a really kind person, but the choice that you have made was not a kind thing to do.'

4. I spotted them being good and spoke about the impact on me and them: 'Sam, it makes me so happy when you are focused and ready to learn, and it will mean that you will get the best out of this lesson.'

Over time, this focus on relationships, and that unconditional positive regard – I valued and appreciated them as individuals and separated them from their behaviour – made a huge impact. The behaviour was still challenging at times, but by the end of the year I was teaching 70 per cent and 30 per cent was behaviour management. (They continued to struggle with the relationships they had with each other.)

Going out of your way to form a relationship is so important. Having those positive relationships means that you build up some social currency, so that when you do have to address challenging behaviour, you can move forward from it quickly.

As you will have seen from the above, the language of choice was also a hugely important factor in managing their behaviour. This gave them ownership. It also allowed me to separate them from their behaviour and provided the opportunity for conversations about choices and consequences. When pupils' behaviour was unacceptable, I would speak to them and ask seven simple questions:

1. What happened?
2. How were you feeling when you…?
3. How are you feeling now?
4. How is X feeling now?
5. Was the choice that you made a kind or unkind one?
6. What could you do differently next time?
7. How can we make this better?

I would then frame the behaviour – for example, 'You chose to hit Barry because you were feeling cross that he took your rubber without asking. Now you are both feeling sad and nothing has improved. Your choice was an unkind one. A better choice would have been to ask politely for it back and I am sure that he would have returned it and you would both be feeling happier. Now you will have to apologise and there will be a consequence for your choice.'

Sometimes there will be an external consequence to a pupil's action following your school's behaviour policy – missed playtime, detention, etc. Parents sign up to these policies by choosing the school. If this is the case, link the consequence to the choice: 'Because you chose to hit someone, it means that you will have to [whatever the policy is].' Again, this removes you personally from the consequence and allows you to keep the relationship intact.

COACHING MOMENT

▶ How confident do you feel building relationships with pupils?

▶ What strategies would work for you to build relationships?

▶ What do you feel about your habits at the moment? Are you on the deadly side or the caring side?

Mr T's NQT/ECT support
@MrTs_NQTs

Develop your meerkat skills! When working with a group, don't forget to 'pop' your head up and survey the room, look for those children doing what you want and praise them. This will let the children know you are always watching and you value your expectations.

♡   ⟲   ♡   ⬆

Preventing issues

Most behaviour management happens before a behaviour incident occurs. This section will provide strategies and ideas about how you can manage behaviour effectively.

■ Rules

Every school has its own behaviour management policy. This will identify the school's values and beliefs when it comes to managing pupil behaviour. It will also contain the school's rules and how these should be reinforced with pupils. The policy will often contain a list of agreed consequences for behaviour incidents (both positive and negative). This policy is always your go-to for how to respond to incidents when they occur. The policy protects you and provides consistency for pupils across the school.

Your school will have rules that help it to run smoothly. These are often overarching ways of behaving: being kind, looking after property, telling the truth, etc. These rules have their place in your classroom, but you may need something more specific.

Class charters are often created as a way for all parties in the classroom to agree a set of 'rules' or responsibilities that they need to uphold.

A class charter needs to be co-created to provide ownership for all parties. Depending on where you are in the academic journey of pupils, the content may vary and the 'rules' that pupils provide will be adapted.

A few things to remember:

> Limit the number of 'rules': I never had more than six – they can quickly get lost and forgotten.

> Keep them positive: What *should* pupils do? (You may have to rephrase the ideas that the pupils suggest.)

> Be authentic: Don't just pay lip service to the class charter.

An example class charter is shown here:

Our Class Charter

We want our class to be a fair and happy place where we can play and learn together.

So we promise to:

Signed:

Some example rules:

> We tuck in our chairs.

> We leave the classroom tidy.

> We are kind to each other.

> We share our ideas.

> We listen to the person speaking.

> We put our hand up to ask a question.

> We remember to say please.

> We keep our mobile phones in our bags.

> We give our work our full attention.

> We are courteous to each other.

I always found it hugely beneficial when working with young pupils to get them to demonstrate what the 'rule' might look like. I would then photograph it and display it alongside the written rule, so that it could act as a clear reminder.

Mr T's NQT/ECT support
@MrTs_NQTs

Decide for this year what your expectations will be for different times of the day. How will children line up? How will they access resources? Be clear on these expectations and stick to them! Children may push to find boundaries; sticking to them lets children know that you mean what you say.

Routines and expectations

I have deliberately put these together, as they go hand in hand. You can't establish routines without expectations and your routines are developed to reinforce and reduce the reminders needed for your expectations.

Behaviour needs to be taught, just like anything else in school. It shouldn't be a guessing game for pupils. We need to be explicit in our expectations and provide opportunities for pupils to practise them, so that they know what acceptable behaviour looks like.

The expectations that you have for behaviour and the routines that you develop are your own. You need to be happy with the behaviour systems and routines in the classroom, and as long as the pupils are safe and can learn, you don't need to conform to the way in which the colleague next door teaches.

I used to work next door to a colleague who insisted that the pupils worked in silence the majority of the time – these were her expectations. For me, I liked a buzz in the classroom, so as long as conversation was purposeful, the pupils were allowed to talk to each other.

■ Establishing routines and expectations

First of all YOU need to know these. What will your routine look like/sound like? How will you 'trigger' your routine? Before starting a routine, plan it out.

Here is an example of how a routine might look:

Every day, pupils will need to line up for assembly. So what do they need to do?

> Tuck in their chairs.

> Move to the door.

> Line up.

Simple!

However, this could be like chuck-out time in a pub on a Saturday night! We need to be specific:

> Tuck in your chair, lifting the legs and placing it down carefully.

> Walk quietly to the door, following the people in front.

> Form a straight line, facing the right way, standing smartly (straight back, arms by their sides – this may need visually modelling) with no voices.

Less simple, but pupils now have a fighting chance of achieving what you expect.

When you know and have refined your expectations, you can introduce them and communicate them effectively to the pupils.

Then comes introduction and rehearsal. The time that you invest now will pay dividends in the future:

'When I say line up for assembly you will:

Tuck in your chair, lifting the legs and placing it down carefully.

Walk quietly to the door following the people in front.

Form a straight line, facing the right way, standing smartly with no voices. Off you go.'

At this point, I would be spotting pupils doing exactly what is expected, in order to praise them specifically:

'Mark – you tucked your chair in perfectly, remembering to lift it and place it down carefully.'

'Sam – you are walking quietly to the line and following sensibly behind the person in front.'

Praising helps to reconfirm what the expectations look like and sound like to pupils – similar to the classroom rules that we spoke about previously.

This links really well to Bandura's 'social learning theory' (1977) and is something that I have used so often in my class. By celebrating the behaviours when we see them, the pupils have a clear role model to follow and can then replicate their behaviour. Find your role models as often as possible; pupils need to know what the behaviour looks like in each other.

If pupils aren't following the expectations, I always find that using a question as a reminder is hugely helpful:

'Sally – how should you be moving to the line?'

One of two things will probably happen: Sally will either stop and self-adjust her behaviour to your expectations or she will look at you blankly. If the second one happens, use the opportunity to repeat and reinforce what she should be doing, using those explicit instructions.

As soon as pupils have carried out the routine once, get them to do it again. Repeat your expectations and see whether they can achieve them more quickly, more quietly or more smoothly.

Spending five to ten minutes each day for the first week practising this can save you so much time in the future. You want to get to the point where all you need to say is 'line up for assembly' and it just happens as if by magic. But it will be that effortful practice to begin with that will get you to this point.

This is the same for any routine, whether it be tidying up or coming to a carpet space for the lesson. Whatever routine you need to teach, plan it – be specific – teach it and rehearse it.

Below is a simple prompt to help you to plan your routines (thanks to Dan Whittaker @Class_Whisperer for inspiring the presentation of this):

Routine	Steps	What will it look like?	What will it sound like?
	Tuck in your chairs	Lifting off the ground, chairs placed down carefully	No squeaking or scraping of chair legs
Lining up	Walk to the line	Sensibly and carefully following the person in front	Voices off
	Make a line	Straight line, standing smart, face forward	Voices off

Here is a space for you to plan your own. You may want to consider:

> transitions between activities

> behaviour during teaching times

> expectations for starting work

> expectations for moving around the room or using equipment

> expectations for group work/paired work/independent work.

Routine	Steps	What will it look like?	What will it sound like?

The same principle applies to any expectations that you want to develop – how pupils should stick their work in their book, how they should behave during teaching times. The most important thing to remember is:

> Know the expectations for yourself first.

> Communicate them clearly to the pupils.

> Practise and rehearse them.

> Praise pupils when they demonstrate the expectation and challenge them when they don't.

When you set your expectations, you need to live by them, value them, reinforce them and never accept anything less than what you ask for.

When pupils become confident with the expectations, encourage them to spot the expectations in others: 'Sam, you are lining up fantastically, you are facing forward, standing smartly and I can't hear your voice. Who can you see that is lining up fantastically?'

Praise is the best way in which you can reinforce and build up positive behaviour in class. As Paul Dix says, 'Why attempt to crush behaviours with punishment when you can grow better ones with love?' (2017, p. 8)

COACHING MOMENT

▶ What expectations are important to you?

▶ How confident are you with explaining and reinforcing your expectations?

Mr T's NQT/ECT support
@MrTs_NQTs

Know your expectations for children's behaviour before you try to communicate them. Plan them, keep them clear and precise, rehearse how you will communicate them and make time for children to practise them. Use specific praise to reinforce them! #YouGotThis

♡   ⟲   ♡   ⬆

Dealing with unwanted behaviour

The hope is that by having clear rules and expectations and carefully practised routines, distressed behaviours will be kept to a minimum. However, as we spoke about earlier in the chapter, we can provide an environment where pupils want to behave and make the right choices but we cannot control their behaviour, and if a pupil becomes dysregulated because of an incident (often outside of your control), distressed behaviours will occur.

As discussed earlier in the chapter, I developed my ability to deal with these more significant behaviour incidents by asking the following questions:

1. What happened?
2. How were you feeling when you…?
3. How are you feeling now?
4. How is X feeling now?
5. Was the choice that you made a kind or unkind one?
6. What could you do differently next time?
7. How can we make this better?

The aim is to restore the relationship between you and the pupil, and the relationship between the pupils. However, most day-to-day behaviour will be low-level, in which case this sort of intervention will feel a bit like trying to crack a nut with a hammer!

We should be trying to find the least intrusive ways in which to manage behaviour, and below are a few suggestions:

> **'The look':** This is a great one to practise in the mirror or on your friends or family! Sometimes a glance over with a raised eyebrow is all you need.

> **A non-verbal gesture:** Finger to your lips or a gesture to sit down, etc.

> **Change your position in the room:** By moving nearer to the pupils who are not demonstrating the desired behaviour, it lets them know you have noticed, but allows you to maintain the flow of your teaching.

> **Tactical pause:** Sometimes, just stopping mid-sentence is all you need.

> **Spot others doing the right thing:** This technique can take training for your brain. You will naturally be drawn to children who are not conforming to your expectations; train your brain to scour the room for someone doing the right thing and praise that child. This becomes easier the more confident you are with what the expected behaviour looks like.

> **A simple reminder:** 'What should you be doing now? Show me.' (Link this back to your behaviour expectations.)

These last two are my personal favourites. They allow me to reinforce behaviour expectations and challenge behaviour in a non-confrontational way. Also, for the last one, if pupils genuinely don't know what they should be doing, it gives them the opportunity to ask.

COACHING MOMENT

▶ What simple, least intrusive strategies have worked well for you in the past?

▶ What strategies have you seen used by others that you might want to implement in your own practice?

▶ When managing unsettled behaviour, have you communicated your expectations clearly to the pupils? Do they know what you expect?

■ Repeated or more extreme behaviour

When more serious incidents happen, it can cause you to become flustered, and finding the right thing to say can be difficult. Behaviour scripts can really help in these situations. They are statements that you can rehearse and deliver in a very measured way. (We want pupils to see that we are comfortable and in control – even if we aren't feeling it.)

These scripts can be pre-prepared and you can just substitute the details. For example:

'[Name of pupil], you have just [description of incident], which is unacceptable in our classroom; you are stopping others from learning. Make a different choice about your behaviour and it will enable you and the rest of our class to learn.'

This is just an example; you may want to incorporate your school's behaviour policy into your scripts:

'[Name of pupil], the behaviour that you have just shown is not acceptable in our class. If you continue to do that, you will have to [description of behaviour policy consequence].'

These scripts can allow you to feel in control of the situation.

Try creating your own and then rehearse these so that when behaviour incidents occur, you can respond in a calm and measured way.

For more serious incidents, your school's policy is your go-to. There should be clear consequences laid out for behaviour incidents. However, the way in which you present these should be with the view of restoring pupils – this may mean that at the time, pupils are too dysregulated to engage with a discussion about their behaviour, so you need to provide time for them to calm down before following the question prompts above. It may also be that you are too dysregulated to deal with the behaviour at that point. It is also OK for you to take a step back, remind them that there will be consequences to their actions, but that you will speak to them later (make sure you do address the behaviour later). The worst thing that you can do is to go into a situation angry – this will not end well for anyone!

Rest assured that these incidents will be few and far between. As a rule, pupils want to please and meet your expectations. As long as you have explained and reinforced these relentlessly, pupils will be able to meet them.

If you are finding a particular pupil's behaviour challenging, reach out to colleagues in the school. It is important that you are part of the process of tackling behaviour – it maintains the relationship between you and the pupil – but the senior leaders and colleagues in your school are there to support you.

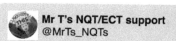 

Mr T's NQT/ECT support
@MrTs_NQTs

As the term goes on, if you start to feel that the pupils are not responding as you'd like to your behaviour techniques, go back to basics with your expectations and really reinforce them again. You will get them back as you want them!

COACHING MOMENT

- ▶ What strategies have you seen that have been used to de-escalate situations?
- ▶ How confident do you feel about managing distressed behaviour in pupils?
- ▶ What could you do to help you feel more confident about managing behaviour?
- ▶ Who in your school would you go to for support with behaviour?

Thoughts from an ECT

Your greatest tool when beginning the school year with your new class is the behaviour management policy. These come in different shapes and sizes but ultimately their job is the same thing: they state the expectations and approach that your school has to behaviour. This can also intertwine with the values that your school wishes to live by and impress upon the children during time at school. This is your base to establishing routines, responses and, most importantly, the strong, positive relationships you have with the children in your class. It is important that the children are being modelled the same message that the school wants to spread, but your style of delivery may differ from your colleagues, just as it does with your day-to-day teaching.

Once you are familiar with the routines to implement in the class, it is time to make the children feel a part of this process. On my first day with a new class, we create a set of class rules that are guided around our whole-school rules. We spend time looking at what actions show that we are following these rules, focusing on how we can demonstrate them throughout the classroom and school. It is important that this is a positively fixed experience so that throughout the year positive examples are referred to and praised every single day. Of course, there will be instances throughout the year where a child or group of children are not meeting the expectations set by the class, but the agreed terms set together will help to guide the restorative conversations so that they are steered back to the high expectations set.

Another tip I have really valued is being consistent with expectations. This word is shared regularly in the teaching profession, but alongside it a word that I have found equally important is 'insistence'. Children are incredibly quick to work out how a teacher responds to behaviour – how far they can push the boundaries in knowing what is acceptable and what is not. The groundwork you do in delivering a consistent and insistent approach to expectations in your first full term will really benefit you as you progress through the year. I have found that treating each child's behaviour in a consistent and fair way has enabled respect to be earned and relationships to be built. A great fear for me going into a new classroom was always 'What if I have to have a difficult conversation about behaviour with a child and they dislike me after it?' However, the expectations being modelled daily, referred to consistently and insisted upon show that I expect the same from every child in our class and that it is a firm but fair message being delivered.

Finally, my last tip is something that I learned on my first placement (from the author of this very book!): the power of impressing upon your peers. Children love praise and they love positivity from their teacher; being told that they are great because they are doing the right thing instantly puts a smile on their face. But, instead of picking out every positive thing that a child does, pick one child displaying a positive behaviour, ask them to find another person in the room doing the same thing, explaining what they are doing, and repeat. You will see straight away a swarm of children sitting up straight, begging to be noticed and asserting themselves towards the expectations set by the class. Not only are they displaying the expectations, but they are also able to recite the expectations in their own words to the whole class. This strategy is just like a smile; it creates a ripple effect and instantly builds the children up to be the best version of themselves whilst feeling great at the same time. You may sound like a broken record, but embedding these expectations and getting the whole class speaking the same language allows for a positive and productive learning environment enshrined in high expectations.

Owen Knight, Primary ECT

Key takeaways

- Our own behaviour has an impact on the learning environment that we create and can have an impact on pupils' behaviour.

- Building relationships is key for behaviour management. Take time to get to know your pupils and allow them to get to know you.

- Most behaviour management happens before an incident occurs. Establishing clear routines and expectations for behaviour promotes positive behaviour.

- When behaviour incidents occur, choosing the right strategy is important, and managing your own emotions is just as important.

CHAPTER 7
CURRICULUM
AND PLANNING

 **Daily tip**

Mr T's NQT/ECT support
@MrTs_NQTs

Be kind to yourself when planning. Don't plan multiple heavy marking sessions on the same day. If you know a lesson will take a lot of prep, try to ensure others around it are quick and easy to resource. Managing workload is so important; do what you can to help yourself.

♡   ⟲   ♡   ⬆

In this chapter we will:

➡ Explore long-term planning and the purpose of this.

➡ Identify how medium-term planning can help you to keep track of the curriculum for pupils.

➡ Look at what you may need to include in short-term/lesson/weekly planning and where to go for inspiration.

Planning is something that I see ECTs asking about support with quite frequently. Most often the questions are about knowing where to start and what needs to be included. In this chapter we will look at a few key strategies that you can use to give you confidence to know that what you are doing is right for you and for your pupils.

Long-term planning

Long-term planning is the overview for the school of what will be taught. The main purpose of long-term planning is to ensure that the expectations and content for the National Curriculum are being covered, alongside RE, PSHE and exam board expectations. The other purpose of long-term planning is to allow parents to know what is being taught and to see how the school curriculum is being implemented.

The primary National Curriculum (DfE, 2013, p. 5) identifies that 'The school curriculum comprises all learning and other experiences that each school plans for its pupils. The national curriculum forms one part of the school curriculum.' Your school will decide the most important knowledge, skills and understanding that pupils need, and the National Curriculum will inform this. When you arrive at the school, the chances are that you will inherit the long-term planning from the previous teacher or school leaders, which will outline what is taught when. However, you may arrive at a school looking to revamp its curriculum, so it is important that you can contribute fully to the conversation.

When constructing a long-term plan, the coverage of the curriculum and the opportunities that pupils need should be identified, and then the 'how' can be identified. The National Curriculum outlines exactly what it is that pupils need to be able to demonstrate by the end of each key stage or year group. These are the skills that pupils need in order to have the opportunities to develop. However, the context of how these will be done is up to you/the school. Most schools will organise their learning through topics that enable the pupils to learn and develop the knowledge, skills and understanding needed. Look at your (potential) school's website – what does the long-term curriculum planning look like?

Let's take, for example, the Key Stage 1 history curriculum. One of the objectives is that pupils should be taught about events beyond living memory that are significant nationally or globally. It provides examples, but ultimately it is up to the school to decide on what these events are. One of the skills that pupils need to develop is to ask and answer questions about the past. Again, this can be done through any content that is felt appropriate.

There are times when things become more specific. Continuing with the history curriculum, in Key Stage 2 pupils must be taught about the Roman Empire and its impact on Britain. There is flexibility about when this is covered in Key Stage 2, but more specific content has been identified. Similarly, in Key

Stage 3, we have the development of the Church, state and society in Britain 1509–1745 – again, very specific content.

However, when we get to English as a focus, there is more of a list of skills that pupils need the opportunity to develop and demonstrate. In writing, the skills range from being able to punctuate simple sentences to considering how their writing reflects the audience and purpose for which it was intended. These skills can be taught through a variety of contexts, and this allows you to show your creativity.

Many schools will use schemes to support them in ensuring the coverage of the curriculum and that pupils develop the skills expected of them. These can be great to help you to ensure that coverage is there, but can also be a little restrictive in terms of how you teach.

RE, RSE and PSHE are all statutory subjects but there is no guidance for them in the National Curriculum. Many local authorities, companies and charities will create their own 'syllabuses' for these subjects that schools can adopt and use.

This is an example from my own experience:

Topic title	Zoom to the moon!	Celebrations!	London's burning	Into the woods	Beside the seaside
Term	Autumn 1	Autumn 2	Spring 1	Spring 2 Summer 1	Summer 2
Possible WOWs/ trips	Alien visitor	Planning a party	Time capsule Burning of houses	Visit to the woods	Seaside visit
Literacy	Alien stories	Religious stories	Diary entries Recounts	Non-chronological reports Traditional tales	Letters and postcards
Maths	See separate curriculum bank				
Science	Materials		Changes in materials	Habitats and plants	Habitats and animals
Computing	Alien art	Programming – firework display	Internet safety	Presenting information	Digital photography
Geography	Identifying features of Earth from above		Locating cities on map of UK	Locating rainforests using globes and atlases	Comparing localities Local area and seaside
History	Famous astronauts	Gunpowder Plot	Great Fire of London		Victorian seasides

Art	Alien pictures	Firework art	Observational drawings of Tudor houses	Camouflage art		Observational drawings of shells
D&T	Build a space rocket	Edible sparklers	Tudor houses	Build a nest or den		Finger puppets
Music	'The Planets' Suite'	Christmas carols	London's Burning	Woodland soundscapes		
RE	Belonging	Celebrations	Leaders and teachers	Believing		
PE	FUN-damentals	FUNdamentals Dance	Gym Games	Games Dance	Gym Games	Outdoor games
PSHE	New beginnings	Getting on and falling out	Going for goals Keeping safe	Good to be me!	Relation-ships	Changes
Weather Week	In each season: explore weather patterns, observe the changes in plants and animals over the year, create a diary noting the changes to the length of day, shadows and physical changes					

COACHING MOMENT

▶ What priorities does your school have for their school curriculum?

▶ What schemes does your school use?

▶ Where does your school draw their curriculum from for RE, PSHE and RSE?

Mr T's NQT/ECT support
@MrTs_NQTs

Daily tip

Your planning is personal to you. If what you plan enables you to teach effective lessons, it can look however it needs to. There may be some expectations from your school. But make sure that it works for you.

♡   ⟲   ♡   ⬆

Medium-term planning

This was always my favourite planning to do. The long-term planning gives you the skeleton of what you will teach, but the medium-term planning starts to add meat to the bones and addresses the 'how'. It will help you to really consider the intention, implementation and intended impact. These may be Ofsted 'buzz words' at the time of writing this, but they are also a really good way to consider your medium-term planning.

> **Intention:** What is it that you want the pupils to learn? This will often be linked to the National Curriculum or syllabus that you are following, but at times there are those more open objectives that you can craft into the areas that inspire and motivate you.

> **Implementation:** How will you get the pupils to learn this? For example, if you want pupils to know the different parts of a flowering plant, what learning opportunities will they need? Why are you teaching them now? What is it that pupils have needed to know before they learn this? How will it support them moving forward? The implementation is your chance to get creative, but also to be able to justify why you have made the decisions that you have.

> **Impact:** What do you intend pupils to get from their learning? How will you know that there has been an impact? What will that impact look like? Impact should not just be considered in relation to the National Curriculum or syllabus objectives, but also to the experiences/context that you offer.

This is an example of a history sequence of three lessons on a topic: 'Zoom to the moon!'

Learning objective: Learn about changes in living memory	Learning objective: Order events chronologically	Learning objective: Learn about the lives of significant individuals in the past
Ask children how we have managed to learn so much about our planet and what it looks like from space. Discuss how space exploration has meant that we have been able to look more closely at Earth and other planets around us. Talk children through the timeline of space exploration and how it has progressed to now planning trips to space as leisure activities. Use the timeline to display in class.	Focus on significant events in space exploration history, e.g. first dog/chimpanzee into space. Create mini information book with chronological pages, using Book Creator on iPads, e.g. first rocket into space, first insect/dog/chimpanzee into space, first man into space and so on.	Focus on significant people in space exploration, e.g. Yuri Gagarin, Neil Armstrong and Buzz Aldrin. Add information pages to the mini booklets on Book Creator.

You can see that there are specific learning objectives identified and a rough outline of the content for the lesson. Differentiation and provision for specific pupils is still not included at this point, but it is clear that pupils will have the opportunity to start to address key objectives and skills identified in the National Curriculum.

There are also opportunities to develop skills from across the curriculum. For example, pupils using technology to communicate their understanding. Whilst this is not the main drive of the learning, the way in which the history objectives have been implemented will clearly have a positive impact on pupils' engagement and on their technology skills: intention, implementation and impact.

Medium-term plans for English and mathematics may look a little different.

For maths, many schools follow the structure of White Rose (https://whiterosemaths.com) or a scheme that outlines when key skills are taught. The White Rose overview is freely available online, and if you find yourself in the position of having to teach mixed-age classes, there is a structure that has been adapted for this.

For English, there is much more flexibility. Some schools will align with topics and English curriculum skills are taught through the topics. For example, with the topic 'Zoom to the moon!', pupils develop their understanding of non-fiction texts through fact files about the planets, engage with narrative by writing about the arrival of an alien – inspired by the book *Beegu* – and look at descriptive writing when creating their own alien.

Alternatively, your school may drive its English work through the use of texts, using a book, poem or excerpt as a stimulus for pupils to develop English skills. If this is the case, it is important to develop your breadth of age-appropriate texts. @MrEPrimary has some incredible book lists, linked to different topics and age groups, that will inspire you.

COACHING MOMENT

- ▶ What do you intend for the pupils to learn? How does this link to the National Curriculum or syllabus being addressed?

- ▶ How will you deliver the teaching? What skills do pupils need to develop? Where do your passion and enthusiasm lie?

- ▶ What impact do you want to have on pupils' learning? What should pupils be able to do by the end of the topic/sequence of learning/year? How will you measure this impact or know that it has been successful?

Mr T's NQT/ECT support
@MrTs_NQTs

Plan a few key questions for each session. Use these to assess children's understanding during the session and then reflect on them at the end. Has children's understanding moved on? Has the quality of their answers improved? This is a quick way to measure progress.

Short-term planning

Here we are at the business end of the planning process. This is where all that information that you have gets distilled down into the lesson that you intend to teach. Let's be clear: every school has different expectations for planning. Some specify a format, whilst some are happy for presentation slides to be the evidence for planning. You may find yourself planning from a rigid scheme or that you are part of a parallel planning team and are given planning for some subjects. Whatever the format or situation, below I outline the thought process that I would always recommend you consider.

■ What am I teaching?

Hopefully this is an obvious one, but one that sometimes gets lost. There are many resource sites out there that provide a whole range of activities, and sometimes these then drive the planning. Remember that you should have a clear learning intention in your mind, and the activities should be a way in which pupils can secure and demonstrate their understanding. When working with ECTs, so often I see lessons where they share the learning objective with the pupils and the activity does not relate or allow the pupils to actually achieve the intended outcomes. When unpicking it afterwards, it usually comes down to 'I thought that they would enjoy the activity'. Enjoyment is a key factor in learning, but ultimately that objective was chosen – usually from the National Curriculum or syllabus. Ensure that you are clear with what the objective looks like and how the activity will enable pupils to demonstrate their understanding of it.

■ How will I know that pupils have achieved the objective?

This links to assessment and how you will assess pupils – see the section below and Chapters 9 and 10 – and also to the clarity of the learning intention: has there been a very specific skill or piece of knowledge that you have intended for pupils to master? This is where your success criteria are developed. As will be discussed in Chapter 8, these provide clarity for the pupils in how they can be successful, and at the end of the lesson or sequence of lessons, you and they will know whether they have been successful in meeting the objective.

■ Who am I teaching?

This is a huge one, especially if you follow a scheme or have planning created for you. These plans will address all aspects of planning except the area related to the pupils themselves. The people who have written the planning may never have met your class of pupils (or you for that matter). This is where you need to consider: Will this work for all my pupils? How might I need to adapt it to provide challenge for some? How might I need to adapt it to provide support for others? There may even be pupils in your class who need pre-teaching before they can even access the content of the session (see Chapter 8). Remember, you know your children the best. Use that knowledge to make your planning work for them.

■ How will I teach the objective?

You know what you are teaching and to whom. But now you need to consider how you will teach it. How will the lesson be structured? What approaches will you use? (See Chapter 11 for some suggestions.) How will you ensure that learning moves at the right pace? These are all complex questions, and the answers will vary depending on what you are teaching. A lesson on developing scientific understanding through an experiment would be structured and delivered very differently to a handwriting lesson. You will find a lesson style that works for you and your children. This is also a good point at which to consider the time that you have for the lesson – don't over-plan and try to cram too much in. Keep the focus tight and you will feel a greater sense of achievement. In other words – do less, better!

■ How will I manage the learners?

Planning key behaviour support strategies can make the difference between an excellent lesson and a car crash! I have seen so many 'wow' lessons that have fallen apart because the expectations for the learners have not been made clear. You may not need to formally record this on your written plan, but if you know that you are using a structure where pupils will be moving around the classroom frequently or engaged in practical or paired work, you must consider what expectations need to be put in place and how you will communicate these to pupils. Taking time to think about these things can make a huge difference to the lesson. You may want to record expectations formally and display them for the pupils, or you may just want to consider them prior to the lesson. See Chapter 6 for how these can be communicated effectively. Either way, it could save you a headache during the lesson!

■ How will I assess the pupils' learning?

You have established the objective and success criteria for the lesson, but how will you assess whether pupils have achieved what you intended? Peer-assessment or self-assessment? Live marking? Observations? Questioning? Hot tasks? However you decide to assess, you also need to consider what you will do with the information. (More detail can be found on these assessment strategies in Chapters 9 and 10.)

As was touched upon in Chapter 4, short-term planning also allows you to take control of your week and ensure that your workload is manageable. I am a huge advocate of looking at the week and considering questions such a, 'Where are my big marking sessions?', 'Which sessions will need more preparation time?' and 'How can I ensure that I am not needing to mark 60 books on staff meeting night when the feedback is needed for the next day?'. Plan your week carefully. Think about the way in which you will assess the pupils and how the activities that you have planned will help you to understand pupils' learning. If assessment can be done practically, do it. If you can engage pupils in peer-/self-assessment, do it. Finding balance to your working week can help you to be more productive as a teacher and give you time and space to think creatively.

COACHING MOMENT

▶ Does your activity allow pupils to demonstrate the learning intention for the lesson?

▶ How have your learners' needs been considered within the lesson?

▶ How will you and your pupils know that they have been successful?

▶ How will you structure and then manage the learners during the lesson?

▶ How can you take control of your week to make it work for you?

Where to look for inspiration

There are many well-known resource sites out there that provide activities and entire curriculums for you to use. Having a range of sites to inspire you can be hugely beneficial – if the wheel has already been invented, why reinvent it?! However, relying on resource sites does not always allow you to teach in a way that is creative or that meets the needs of you, your school or your pupils. Ready-made activities and ideas should always come with a word of caution – you must adapt them to suit your children and your way of teaching. In the past, I have wasted time trawling for a very specific type of activity to allow pupils to develop their understanding, when it would have been quicker to make my own!

Here are some of my go-to sites for inspiration:

> **Pobble365:** This provides an image for each day of the year to be used as a stimulus for discussion, inference or writing. There are suggested ideas provided by the site to help get you started.

> **The Literacy Shed:** This provides a huge range of stimuli to inspire you and your pupils, including images, extracts and short videos, along with accompanying plans and ideas.

> **Nrich.maths.org:** This contains a huge range of practical activities and problems that are carefully aligned to the National Curriculum objectives for maths.

> **NCETM:** The National Centre for Excellence in the Teaching of Mathematics has a great site, with fluency, reasoning and problem-solving activities for all areas of mathematics. There are also some great CPD opportunities shared on here.

> **Social media:** Pinterest, Twitter, Instagram, Facebook – these are all places where teachers share their time and resources to inspire others (particularly useful for those Christmas, Easter and seasonal craft ideas).

> **TES:** This is another place where teachers share their ideas and activities that could provide a source of inspiration for you. Some are free and some have to be paid for.

Thoughts from an ECT

A school's curriculum design reflects the vision for how their children will learn successfully. Drawing on the National Curriculum, and in some cases guidance from Ofsted, schools determine the knowledge and skills that they wish for their children to master, often aligning the school's ethos around this. With this in mind, it is important to understand the key values and ethos of the school/MAT in which you work, as this will underpin their curriculum intent.

Having taught in different schools for my first and second years as an ECT, I have experienced two contrasting ways of designing and implementing curriculum. One focused heavily on a skills-led curriculum, where the children were taught skills explicitly through planned lessons or activities. This resulted in an emphasis on growth mindset, building resilience and other such learning behaviours. In another school, the focus was a knowledge-led approach, where the curriculum was designed around clear subject knowledge and a deep understanding of concepts. Designing such a curriculum requires planning for progression year on year, so that children can link a concept taught in, say, Year 1 to a similar one in Year 5. Whilst both approaches certainly have their merits, in my experience working towards a knowledge-rich curriculum has provided excellent learning outcomes for my class, as well as an ability to connect ideas in unexpected ways – this term it was linking the idea of tyrannical leaders in the 1600s to various current world leaders. Their ability to make such connections required a deep conceptual understanding of the subject and an ability to apply this knowledge.

When designing your curriculum, build on prior knowledge and sequence lessons effectively so that children are able to build on foundational knowledge in order to study more complex tasks. Where these links are tenuous, children can develop misconceptions, which, if not addressed swiftly, can become embedded in their thinking. I found that this particularly occurred in maths, and began to detail key misconceptions in my planning, both short- and medium-term. Including these in planning helped me not only to determine how each lesson or lesson sequence needed to be designed but also to pre-plan potential pitfalls and how to navigate these successfully. I often scribble notes on any medium-term plans I have when something new crops up, in order to be able to plan more effectively in subsequent lessons/years.

Most importantly – ask questions. You will likely have a roadmap from your school on how they wish for the children to learn, but the best resources will be your teaching colleagues. If I could give myself any advice for those first few months, it would be to ask questions, have a look at others' planning, speak to subject leads, and make sure you understand why things are designed as they are. This will give you an excellent foundation on which to create an engaging curriculum for your amazing young people.

Rachel Speake, Primary ECT

Key takeaways

- Long-term planning provides the structure for you to ensure curriculum coverage.

- Medium-term planning allows you to consider the intention, implementation and impact of what you do, and to get creative.

- Short-term planning should be focused on the pupils, and lessons need to be carefully aligned to give the greatest chance of a successful outcome.

- Having a few key websites to go to for inspiration can be great – but make sure that you don't lose too much time trawling these instead of crafting your own activities.

- Short-term planning should work for you – use it to help you get the most from your pupils and to help with managing your workload.

CHAPTER 8

MEETING THE NEEDS OF ALL

Daily tip

Mr T's NQT/ECT support
@MrTs_NQTs

Sometimes you need to ask children before displaying their work.
If children are not happy with what they have done (even if you are),
displaying it for all to see can be the worst thing possible for them.
#YouGotThis

In this chapter we will:

➡ Establish the importance of knowing your pupils and the strategies that we can use to get to know them.

➡ Explore strategies for quality-first teaching, to meet the needs of pupils.

➡ Begin to understand specific SEND needs and how we can start to build our understanding of how to meet these needs.

When we talk about meeting the needs of all, it can be a daunting prospect. There are 30 individuals in each lesson, each with different banks of prior knowledge and experiences, with different attitudes to learning and with different external factors that will influence their capacity for learning in that moment. This has led me to the conclusion that meeting the needs of all should be thought of as a long-term aim, and not a short-term goal.

Know your pupils

To be able to meet the needs of your pupils, you must know *what* your pupils need. You will be building up your knowledge of your pupils all the time, but for some pupils you will need to formalise the way in which you gather information in order to help you understand them and what they can do.

In order to gather information on pupils, you can:

 Watch them: What are they doing? How do they approach the tasks and work that you ask them to do?

 Listen to them: What are they saying? When in discussion with others, what is their verbal communication like?

 Speak to them: Ask them what helps them to learn. What makes things more challenging/tricky for them?

 Think about them: When you are outside of the classroom, take time to ponder on them. Why did they struggle with that? What else do I know about them? I used to have my biggest epiphanies about children when outside on playground duty or sat in the staff room.

In considering the needs of your pupils, you may wish to consider these questions:

> What are their strengths?

> What can they do already?

> What do they enjoy?

> What triggers a reaction?

> What calms them?

> What helps them to focus?

> What distracts them?

The majority of these questions are focused on the positives – what pupils 'can do'. This gives you a starting point on which to build. Also, it helps you, and others, to see pupils in a positive light. So often I have sat in SEND review meetings and heard repeatedly what a child is unable to do. Find the positives and build on these.

COACHING MOMENT

▶ What do you know about the pupils who puzzle you the most?

▶ How confident do you feel about knowing those pupils' strengths?

Mr T's NQT/ECT support
@MrTs_NQTs

Daily tip

Remember, not all pupils will arrive in your room with the same prior knowledge and experiences. Visiting the beach or knowing the name of a farm animal can be key gaps for some pupils. Take time to plug the gaps and don't assume all children have had the same opportunities.

Strategies to support pupils

With such a complex range of pupils in front of us, there are some approaches that you can invest in that are good practice for all pupils. Quality-first teaching was introduced in the current SEND Code of Practice (DfE and DHSC, 2015) and emphasises how important the way in which we teach is for meeting the needs of all, with the principle being that by improving our general practice, we reduce the need to adapt for specific students.

The following strategies are ways in which we can adapt practice to make our teaching as inclusive as possible.

■ Visual timetable

If you haven't got one, get one. These are deemed good practice for children with learning needs, such as those with an autistic spectrum condition (ASC), but they work well for everyone. They let children know what is happening, help them to emotionally and mentally prepare for what is coming during the day, and stop them asking 'When will it be lunchtime?' in the middle of your phonics session.

■ A clear, shared learning objective

It doesn't matter how learning objectives are structured; take time to share them at some point during the session, and explain them to the children if necessary. If everybody knows and understands what they are expected to learn/know/understand/be able to do by the end of the lesson, it will help you to focus your teaching to enable everyone to get there, and also help the children to know where it is you want them to be by the end of the lesson.

■ Success criteria

When planning your lesson, success criteria can be a key checklist for you to utilise in order to ensure that you and, ideally, the children have a clear understanding of how you can meet the learning objective. I always think of success criteria as a recipe.

Sometimes you need the ingredients: capital letters, full stops, adjectives and conjunctions (when completing a piece of writing).

Sometimes you need the step-by-step instructions: first add together the ones numbers. If you have more than ten, exchange ten ones for one ten and then add together the tens – don't forget any extras that you have made from the ones (when introducing column addition in maths).

These success criteria help to focus your adaptations for pupils.

What parts will students need more support with? (A word mat for adjectives, Dienes equipment in maths.)

How can I shape my tasks to allow all the children to succeed? (Variation in numbers utilised, pictures to help children generate sentences.) It can also help to shape your teaching…

■ Differentiation

This is a term that has been around for while and has recently come under scrutiny. However, it is a term you will still hear frequently and as part of a wider view of adaptive teaching it can still be beneficial to consider the three types of differentiation:

❯ Differentiation by task: How will you adapt the task for children?

> Differentiation by support: What support will enable them to get there? (Adult support, peer support, concrete apparatus, word mat, etc.)

> Differentiation by outcome: Everyone will do the same task, but what they produce will be different.

Within a lesson, you may have one, two or all three of these, but remember that whatever support you offer, it should be support that will enable the pupils to meet the learning objective – rather than complete the task – that you set out at the start.

Modelling

As a teacher, I have strutted my stuff down a catwalk many a time. Clearly I jest, unless you count the World Book Day assemblies when, as teachers, we had to show off our costumes, but children need to see processes being modelled. This is something that even more experienced teachers I have worked with shy away from at times (particularly in observed lessons), but is something that is so vital for the children. Live modelling in particular allows pupils to watch a shared piece of work coming together, and the shared writing process can be hugely beneficial to all children. It not only allows them to see the finished product, but also allows you to model the thinking process involved in writing. I always had children with whiteboards on the carpet and at times would ask them to write down example adjectives that could work or a whole sentence that could be included, to keep children engaged in the learning process. We often assume that children know what we mean when we ask them to do something – in my experience, this often leads to multiple regathering of the children to explain again. Save yourself some time and energy by ensuring that expectations have been explained and the processes modelled effectively before asking the children to start the activity.

Flexible grouping

I led our school away from 'ability grouping' about ten years ago. It was met with resistance at first – often to do with how much harder it would make the teachers' lives. In reality, what happened was that when teachers tried grouping children based on the previous lesson, or adapting groups during the lesson, they found that the children were gaining more success; the 'lower attainers' were no longer grouped together, incapacitated until the adult arrived to support them, and children were no longer restricted by what others who were in the same group as them were expected to do. Ability groups are often dictated by how well pupils have performed in the first few sessions of English and maths, and then that's it; that's the group they are in for science, geography, PSHE, etc. Pupils should be grouped by need, but doing this flexibly day to day allows you to truly make sure that pupils are getting the opportunities that they need, and not just the default task because of the table on which they are sitting.

Here are two examples in action. When teaching writing, children sat in mixed-ability groups on the first day. After reviewing their work that evening, they were regrouped based upon their needs; some needed support with the structure of their writing, and some with developing more complex sentence structures. These children then received focused teaching to address their needs, whilst the others could continue with their work. In maths, children would be regrouped each day; some needed to go back a step and utilise more concrete methods, whilst others needed moving on. The way in which I planned never changed and the opportunities that I needed to prepare hadn't increased. What had changed was the targeted support that children received, and they were no longer pre-judged because they were in 'red group'.

■ Learning resources

What support tools do you use in the classroom – word mats, vocab sheets, manipulatives in mathematics? Are these materials available to all pupils? Often, we provide these prompts to those pupils who may be finding the current learning a challenge. However, by having them clearly labelled in the classroom and freely available to all, we can boost not only pupils' achievement but also their independence in learning.

Mr T's NQT/ECT support Daily tip
@MrTs_NQTs

Towards the end of term start thinking about what has worked in the classroom. Which displays have children engaged with? Which systems have worked well? Which resources have had the biggest impact? If you're not sure, ask the pupils!

■ Multiple models of representation

As teachers, we rely on our ability to verbally explain many of the expectations that we have for pupils. However, for some pupils this is too much information to hold in their working memories, and they can struggle to understand what we are explaining. The use of simple visuals or visual prompts can act as a reminder for pupils and reduce the impact on their working memory. By providing information, concepts and processes both visually and orally, we can make a huge impact.

For example, when reading, we may come across a great piece of vocabulary that we want the pupils to remember. We might explore it through discussion;

we may even write the word on the board (drawing an image to represent the word provides another way for children to create a mental model of the word and its meaning). By adding this word to the working wall (these are discussed in Chapter 3), and through using the word and the visual, we increase the likelihood of this word being remembered, as pupils have a greater understanding of its meaning and use.

■ Pre-teaching

Pre-teaching can be very valuable – for example, when working with pupils who have English as an additional language (EAL). It is possible that some pupils with EAL will arrive at your lesson with limited prior knowledge or experiences on which to draw. In a science lesson, for example, we may be using some scientific or technical vocabulary. Utilising your or a support staff's time for the first five minutes of a session can enable pupils to access the lesson and achieve the outcome because we have removed the barrier created by their lack of exposure to language/experiences. For example, it could be that you are introducing the pupils to parts of a plant; pupils who are learning with EAL may not know the word 'plant' or the word 'flower'. Spending time showing visual images with the words written underneath in both English and their first language (if the pupils are able to read in their first language) can allow the pupil to more confidently engage with the session.

COACHING MOMENT

▶ What quality-first teaching strategies are you currently utilising in your teaching?

▶ What additional strategies could you use that will have the biggest impact on pupils?

Children with SEND

I could write a whole book about how to support individuals with a special education need and/or disability (SEND) and still not scratch the surface of the complexity of needs that are out there and how each child is an individual and will vary from the next. When planning for SEND pupils, I always start with what they can do. What are their strengths? How can I use these to help them to address their next steps? For some children, building independence can be a key skill; for others, it can be through repeated retrieval of key skills. You know your children far better than I do. Look at any associated paperwork: education, health and care plans (EHCPs) and individual education plans (IEPs) – or whatever name your school gives to them. Speak to previous teachers, TAs and the SENDCo – no one will expect you to know everything that there is to know. What your school should expect is that you are trying things out and reviewing their effectiveness. For example, you may try presenting their work on a different coloured piece of paper to reduce visual stress, or increasing the font size, or providing them with a specific manipulative in maths. Did that work today? Did they achieve what I wanted them to? If yes, try the same process again (don't be disheartened if it doesn't work the second time – children are complex individuals). And if it didn't work, well, you have successfully found a method that doesn't work for that child, and that is important information that you can pass on to the child's next teacher. Having taught for nearly 18 years, I can honestly say that every time I work with a child with more complex SEND needs, I learn more from them than they learn from me. As teachers, it is about us being open to that learning and not being afraid to take a risk and try something new. I once worked with a child who had to sing a song to help him remember how to spell his name. We tried this as we found that he could remember song lyrics (starting with his strength) and then used this strength to help him to achieve his next step – to be able to spell his first name correctly.

■ Expectations for you as an ECT

If you have a pupil with an identified SEND need in your class, you will be given lots of information about them. Their EHCP will provide you with their very broad needs and what support they are entitled to. Not all pupils with an identified SEND need will have an EHCP, but they will have received precise targets from their previous teacher, and these will be captured in a document – possibly called an IEP or 'my plan' (schools have different names for the same document). You will have a transition meeting with the previous class teacher, where you can find out as much as possible about those individuals that you have in your class.

For all pupils with SEND, you will be expected to feed back on the targets that they have been set in review meetings with parents and the SENDCo. If a child has an EHCP, they will have an annual review, which you may be asked to attend. You will usually complete a report before this meeting and there will be other external agencies there too. Educational psychologists, health care professionals and social workers can all be present, depending on the identified needs of the pupil and the type of support that they require.

If during your year you begin to have concerns that a pupil in your class may need more support, beyond what you can offer them as part of your normal classroom practice, it is important that you reach out to your SENDCo and have a discussion about the needs of that pupil. The SENDCo will want to know what things you have tried that have or have not worked, their strengths and the areas that they find challenging. This will start the ball rolling; initially, it may just be a case of monitoring the pupil more closely for a while, but it could also lead to the pupil needing more specific support further down the line. Remember that your role is not to diagnose, but it is to identify and share your concerns.

■ Specific learning needs

Sometimes pupils may arrive to you with an identified specific learning difficulty (SpLD). This is defined in the SEND Code of Practice (DfE & DHSC, 2015, p. 98) as follows:

> 'SpLD affect one or more specific aspects of learning. This encompasses a range of conditions such as dyslexia, dyscalculia and dyspraxia.'

Over the years, I have taught pupils with various 'labels', and over that time I have learned that the label gives you a fraction of the information that you need about the pupil. Each child that arrives to you is unique; however, sometimes having a SpLD label can give you a starting point from which to begin to meet the pupil's needs.

In the upcoming section, I will share some aspects that pupils with a given 'label' may experience, and some suggested starting points for strategies to try. This list is not exhaustive and it should not be used to 'diagnose' pupils (only an educational psychologist or medical doctor can do this). The sections that follow are there to give you a starting point, to help you to understand the needs of the pupils in your class and to provide ideas for strategies that you can try out to support those needs. Please remember that all children with SEND are different. Get to know them and find the strategies that work for them.

Mr T's NQT/ECT support
@MrTs_NQTs

Daily tip

When setting targets for children with SEND, keep them small and tightly focused. Instead of 'recognise all letter sounds', pick five for them to work on and when you want them to recognise them: should they be able to recognise them on flash cards or within words? This makes it easier to know when a target is met.

■ Attention deficit hyperactivity disorder (ADHD)

Attention deficit hyperactivity disorder (ADHD) is a neurological disorder that can affect attention and impulse control and cause excessive motor activity.

It is contained under the umbrella of 'Cognition and Learning' in the SEND Code of Practice (DfE and DHSC, 2015).

It is believed to have both genetic and environmental links. It affects around four in every 100 pupils and is approximately three times more common in boys than in girls.

The disorder itself can have a significant impact on the child's social, emotional and mental health.

Signs

> craving attention

> needing to move around constantly

> struggling to take turns in conversation – blurting out responses

> difficulty in following instructions

> lacking fine motor control

> having trouble with activities that require a sequence of steps

> being disruptive to others

> struggling to maintain attention until completion

> can be easily overstimulated in activities or with the anticipation of activities to come

> a need to fiddle/wriggle whilst listening

> easily distracted/unable to avoid distractions

> prone to daydreaming

> has difficulty sleeping/poor-quality sleep.

NB: For ADHD to be present, symptoms should have begun before the age of six and have been displayed for more than six months.

How it feels

Have a look at this from the ADHD Collective (2017) for an idea of how it feels to have ADHD:

🖑 **https://adhdcollective.com/what-does-it-feel-like-to-have-adhd**

Strategies

> Be consistent with behavioural expectations.

> Learn to spot frustration levels in the child (and yourself) and know when different actions may need to be taken or when to step away.

> Build your awareness of the needs – support the rest of the class in understanding them.

> Provide specific opportunities for being active.

> Let go of the little things – allow children to read lying down or write standing up.

> Never ignore a child's demands – always acknowledge the demand, but make it clear if the time is not appropriate. Remember to always go back to them when it is an appropriate time.

> Use lots of praise for expected behaviours.

> Make work expectations clear – use timers and give a clear indication of the amount to be completed in the time.

> Sit them near the front to avoid distractions from others.

> Surround them with positive role models.

> Use a quiet/secret signal to let them know if behaviours are not appropriate.

> Avoid being overly critical and do not withhold class rewards such as school trips. (The anticipation of the withholding of rewards can make behaviours worse.)

> Minimise overstimulation.

> Provide appropriate 'fiddle toys', such as sticky tack or a soft toy (avoid anything noisy).

Useful resources

https://youngminds.org.uk (support for parents and resources to support children with their mental health)

www.adhdfoundation.org.uk/information/schools (specific support for schools)

www.adhdvoices.com (ADHD from the perspective of children – provides great videos)

Wider reading

Cooper, P. and Bilton, K. (2002), *Attention Deficit/Hyperactivity Disorder: A Practical Guide for Teachers* (2nd edn). London: David Fulton.

Smith, M. (2012), *Hyperactive: The Controversial History of ADHD*. London: Reaktion.

■ Autism spectrum disorder/condition (ASD/ASC)

Autism is a neurological disorder that particularly affects an individual's ability to communicate and interact with the world around them.

It is contained under the umbrella of 'Communication and Interaction' in the SEND Code of Practice (DfE and DHSC, 2015), but pupils with ASC can also have needs contained under 'Cognition and Learning' in the Code of Practice.

ASC covers a wide spectrum of needs, ranging from those that require little support to those that need intensive long-term support, due to being unable to communicate and having limited awareness of the existence of others.

Signs

> a fascination or 'fixation' with a specific object or theme

> a need for routine and structure and struggling when these change

> an inability to understand social cues and pick up on a tone of voice

> a lack of awareness of danger

> an inability to communicate effectively – either repeating key words, phrases or sounds they like or displaying poor communication skills

> becoming frustrated when they are unable to make their needs known

> suffering from sensory overload and becoming distressed by loud noises or intense smells

> struggling to form meaningful social relationships, and those that are formed are often focused on a shared interest (when the friendship moves away from the interest, they struggle to cope)

> limited eye contact

> an inability to lie (the world is a factual place)

> enjoying consistency and objects that have permanence

> can have specific talents, such as a highly developed visual memory and the ability to draw complex scenes from memory.

How it feels

Have a look at this video from the BBC (2018) for an idea of how it feels to have autism:

👆 **www.bbc.co.uk/news/av/uk-45762016**

Strategies

> Use visual timetables and establish clear routines. When routines need to be changed, prepare children in advance.

> Utilise non-verbal communication, such as sign language and visual cue cards, and keep instructions clear and precise.

> Where possible, incorporate children's interests to aid engagement in tasks or use the interests as a reward – 'If you can do three questions, then you can spend five minutes playing with the cars'.

> Do not 'force' children to make eye contact.

> Children may benefit from their own workspace, free from distractions – some may even prefer to wear noise-cancelling headphones to block out classroom noise.

> Identify and celebrate children's talents.

> When asking children to engage in social situations, make their role clear.

> Avoid using statements that could be ambiguous or cause confusion, such as metaphors – I once told the children that they could draw on things around the room to help them…!

> Keep calm and patient – the world can appear a strange and busy place for a child with ASC. They may need to maintain habits that enable them to feel safe, such as clinging to their favourite toy to regain control.

> Use Social Stories™ to support children in making sense of a situation or to help support them in being independent.

Useful resources

👆 **www.nice.org.uk/guidance/cg128/resources (guidance on the signs and symptoms of ASC)**

👆 **www.autism.org.uk/about/strategies/social-stories-comic-strips.aspx (all about Social Stories™)**

👆 **www.autism.org.uk/about/strategies/visual-supports.aspx (provides visual support aids)**

🖑 **https://reachoutasc.com/preparing-an-autism-friendly-classroom/ (explores how to create an ASD-friendly classroom)**

Wider reading

Droney, C. and Verbiest, A. (2021), *The Everyday Autism Handbook for Schools*. London: Jessica Kingsley Publishers.

Hanbury, M. (2012), *Educating Students on the Autistic Spectrum: A practical guide* (2nd edn). London: SAGE.

■ Dyscalculia

Dyscalculia is a neurological disorder that particularly affects an individual's ability to recognise numbers and mathematical representations and to remember the right sequence of steps when calculating.

It is contained under the umbrella of 'Cognition and Learning' in the SEND Code of Practice (DfE and DHSC, 2015).

It is estimated that one in every 20 people has some form of dyscalculia, and people of all intellectual abilities can be affected by it.

Signs

> having a poor sense of numbers, size and distances

> appearing slow when making simple calculations

> panicking in maths sessions and possibly becoming disruptive

> experiencing difficulty in remembering even simple calculations

> struggling to remember times tables

> being unable to visualise and distinguish similar-looking numbers, such as 6 and 9

> being unable to tell the time on an analogue clock

> an inability to recognise small numbers without having to count along

> difficulty in visualising.

How it feels

Have a look at this from The Understood Team (2016) for an idea of what it feels like to have dyscalculia:

🖐 https://tinyurl.com/y5vmverf

Strategies

➤ Break problems down into smaller, more manageable chunks.

➤ Use clear visual prompts and success criteria to support the pupil.

➤ Explore a range of concrete resources to support the pupil in solving calculations and see which works best for them.

➤ Use a multisensory approach to learning.

➤ Teach pupils at their own pace.

➤ Carry out lots of recaps of prior learning.

➤ Remind pupils of the task part-way through their learning.

➤ Avoid putting pupils on the spot in maths lessons.

➤ Praise achievements regularly.

➤ Provide extra time in maths assessments or tests and try to create an environment that feels positive.

➤ Verbally share reminders of timings for activities; don't rely on children being able to keep track of the time.

Useful resources

🖐 www.mathematicalbrain.com (this is the website of Brian Butterworth, who is the UK's leading expert on dyscalculia)

🖐 www.mathsexplained.co.uk/topics.php (contains some free videos on how to teach mathematical concepts)

🖐 http://scotens.org/sen/resources/dyslexia_leaflet_maths.pdf (a guide for supporting students with dyscalculia)

Wider reading

Bird, R. (2017), *The Dyscalculia Toolkit: Supporting learning difficulties in maths* (3rd edn). Los Angeles: SAGE.

Chinn, S. J. and Ashcroft, J. R. (2007), *Mathematics for Dyslexics: Including dyscalculia* (3rd edn). Chichester: John Wiley.

■ Dyspraxia

Dyspraxia is a neurological disorder that particularly affects an individual's movement and coordination.

It is contained under the umbrella of 'Cognition and Learning' in the SEND Code of Practice (DfE and DHSC, 2015).

It is believed to affect one in every 30 children, with a ratio of four to one of boys to girls. It is not fully understood what causes dyspraxia, but it is believed to stem from a disruption in the way in which the brain communicates with the body. Children with dyspraxia are often of average or above-average intelligence.

Signs

> general clumsiness – falling over fresh air

> slow and hesitant in most actions

> limited spatial awareness – trying to squeeze themselves into spaces that are too small, or frequently bumping into furniture or others

> hands become tired quickly when writing or drawing

> struggle to cross the midline of the body, e.g. touch their left knee with their right hand

> did not crawl as an infant or had delays in key milestones

> poor short-term memory

> poor organisational skills

> struggles with self-care – dressing, undressing, toileting and so on

> struggles with skipping, hopping, catching and kicking a ball

> could struggle to coordinate arms and legs when running – may move the same side arm and leg together rather than the opposite

> may have poor speech

> poor attention span and tendency to fiddle.

How it feels

Have a look at this post from Natalie Williams (2015) for an idea of what it feels like to have dyspraxia:

🖑 **https://theblogwithonepost.wordpress.com/2015/01/17/31**

Strategies

> Break down tasks into small, manageable chunks.

> Ensure that the child's chair is the right height, with both feet flat on the floor and knees at a 90-degree angle – this should be the case for when children are eating as well as working.

> A writing slope or sticking paper to the desk using masking tape when writing may be of benefit to some children.

> Create clear accessible pathways around the classroom.

> Reduce or limit the amount of handwriting that the pupil must do.

> Some children may benefit from having the back of their chair touching a wall.

> Encourage engagement in sports activities, but pair them with children who have patience.

> Provide focused physical/occupational therapy-type activities – for example, programmes such as Fizzy or SMART moves.

> Encourage engagement in repetitive dance or aerobic sequences daily – this can help to build stronger neural pathways.

> Adapt equipment where possible – for example, provide pencil grips and slower-moving or easy-to-grip equipment in PE.

> Provide a visual timetable with reminders of the key equipment that is needed for each session.

Useful resources

https://dyspraxiafoundation.org.uk (key website with links to films about dyspraxia)

www.ot-mom-learning-activities.com (provides practical activities for supporting specific fine- and gross-motor activities)

www.dfyouth.org.uk (website for supporting young people with dyspraxia)

Wider reading

Boon, M. (2010), *Understanding Dyspraxia: A Guide for Parents and Teachers* (2nd edn). London: Jessica Kingsley Publishers.

Drew, S. and Atter, E. (2008), *Can't Play Won't Play: Simply sizzling ideas to get the ball rolling for children with dyspraxia*. London: Jessica Kingsley Publishers.

■ Dyslexia

Dyslexia is a neurological disorder that particularly affects an individual's ability to acquire and process language.

It is contained under the umbrella of 'Cognition and Learning' in the SEND Code of Practice (DfE and DHSC, 2015).

Ten per cent of the population have mild to severe dyslexia. Difficulties can range from poor spelling or an inability to read with an age-appropriate fluency to impact on working memory, gross-motor coordination and personal organisation.

Signs

> spelling the same word in different ways throughout a piece of writing

> being articulate and verbally strong, but unable to record ideas in writing

> struggling with reading fluency

> limited understanding of what they read but a good understanding of what is read to them

> reversals or confusion of letters, particularly b, d and p

> frustration and anxiety in English sessions – can lead to disruptive behaviour/ avoidance tactics

> sounds in words recorded in the wrong order – for example, 'top' instead of 'pot'

> incorrect selection of graphic representation of phonemes – for example, 'phrog' instead of 'frog'

> struggling to continue a rhyming string

> omitting or changing the suffix in words – for example, 'need' instead of 'needed'

> 'loses' letters in clusters – for example, 'thee' instead of 'three' or 'stig' instead of 'string'.

NB: The signs can often be stages that young children go through when learning language. Because of this, most assessments will not take place below the age of seven.

How it feels

'Imagine you are living in a world where you can confidently see, hear and talk to those around you, but when you are asked to read or write anything you feel that you have been transported to another planet.' (Irving and Martin-Denham, in Martin-Denham, 2015, p. 111)

There are some very helpful fonts, created by the designer Daniel Britton, that simulate the level of frustration that a person with dyslexia would experience when trying to read on the following website:

 www.designweek.co.uk/inspiration/dyslexia-typeface-by-daniel-britton/

Strategies

❯ Avoid black text on a white background to reduce visual stress – tweak the background colour on computer screens and interactive whiteboards.

❯ Select simple, clean fonts for typed work.

❯ Provide coloured overlays to children (the colour that works best for them will vary) to make their usual reading books accessible.

❯ Allow children to record their ideas on coloured paper (again, children's preferences for colour will vary).

❯ Use rhymes and mnemonics to aid children with spelling.

❯ Utilise mind-mapping skills to help children to remain organised.

❯ When writing on whiteboards, ensure that words are well spaced and that any other annotations and marks, such as underlining, are made in a different colour (to avoid confusion).

❯ Allow alternative ways for children to present their work, such as the use of a voice-to-text recorder, pictures or music.

❯ Allow additional time for children to read what is presented to them.

❯ Utilise resources that allow children to be independent, such as word books and vocabulary mats.

❯ Use a visual timetable.

❯ Using colour-coding to identify different parts of a sentence – for example, full stops, capital letters and different word types.

Useful resources

www.bdadyslexia.org.uk (the website of the British Dyslexia Association)

https://paper.li/troyka/1306322294# (a weekly round-up of dyslexia news and information)

www.dyslexia.uk.net/dyslexia-in-children (provides a checklist of the signs of dyslexia in primary-aged children)

https://chattalearning.com/dyslexia-friendly-classroom/ (ideas for creating a dyslexia-friendly classroom)

Wider reading

Hall, W. (2009), *Dyslexia in the Primary Classroom*. Exeter: Learning Matters.

Reid, G. (2012), *Dyslexia and Inclusion: Classroom approaches for assessment, teaching and learning* (2nd edn). Oxford: Routledge.

COACHING MOMENT

▶ Who are your pupils with SEND?

▶ What do you know about them?

▶ What are their strengths and interests?

▶ What strategies will you try in order to meet their needs?

Thoughts from an ECT

Having completed my PGCE a little later – I had an undergraduate degree in psychology and experience of working in various children's emotional health and SEND settings to support me with my understanding of meeting the needs of all in the classroom – I was passionate to bring my values surrounding inclusion into my teaching. However, as a trainee teacher, I remember thinking to myself, 'How is it going to be possible for me, with a class of 30 children, to meet the needs of *all* children, when everyone's needs are so different?'

When we talk about meeting the needs of all, we think of the buzzwords and phrases: 'inclusion', 'differentiation' and 'challenging our greater-depth children'. Often, people's ideas of differentiation are to provide different activities for different groups of children and for their classroom to be organised into tables of set abilities. However, not only is this time-consuming to be planning different activities or making multiple different worksheets for every lesson, but it also begs the question, 'Is this really inclusion?'

Inclusion, for me, simply means to include everybody: a collaborative experience of embarking on a journey of learning together. And therefore, I believe that the most valuable tool for differentiation in the classroom is *you*, the teacher. By adapting and carefully planning your lessons, you can bring all children on the learning journey with you – and the first step to this is instilling confidence.

Often, when facing a new challenge, even as an adult, it is common for us to feel a little nervous or anxious about our ability to succeed. However, if you feel successful from the very beginning, no matter how small that step may be, you are more likely to be engaged, feel confident in your ability and be motivated to take on further challenges. This is where you provide 'scaffolding' for children to feel successful, and I have done this by using tactile manipulatives or hands-on resources and experiences, playing fun quizzes or games, generating ideas verbally and collating them together and asking pupils questions to make links to their own lives or experiences.

Once all children are engaged, confident and motivated, this is where I implement small, incremental steps, to increase challenge and deepen understanding. This is where I believe that you, as the teacher, are the best differentiator, as you can use effective questioning to deepen understanding and challenge all your children at an appropriate level.

Therefore, as well as instilling confidence and teamwork mentality in the classroom, it is also important to promote growth mindset and a positive approach to challenge. This is something that my class are currently working on, as they are often apprehensive about pushing themselves outside of their comfort zone. We refer to and discuss a visual diagram of the 'comfort zone', 'challenge zone' and 'danger zone'. The children respond well to this and can make links to their own experiences straight away; this way, we reinforce a positive attitude to challenge and recognise that challenge is different for all of us. By doing this, all children can aim for success and seek challenge, and there are no 'ceilings' placed on any child's learning. This is an exciting concept because children will blow you away with their abilities and hidden talents.

We use mixed-ability learning partners, which is a great way in which to support children who find learning more challenging, but also to encourage children working at greater depth to deepen their understanding of the learning, as you have to really understand a concept to be able to support someone else and explain it to them. It is also a great way of boosting the confidence of your lower-ability learners and SEND children. In our class, we change learning partners each week and use lots of pair-talk to support children in their learning and to allow all children to explore ideas and have their voices heard.

Another way I work to meet the needs of all children is with my classroom set-up and environment. We are all different types of learners and have different ways of learning best. I always aim to provide multisensory learning, as this a great way of engaging all children. Visual supports (like images, widgets and timetables) are not only great supportive aids for children with SEND needs, but they can also help to reduce anxiety and support understanding in *all* children in the class. Using visual supports consistently across the classroom, and through the learning, has supported my children to make connections with their learning and enable understanding.

Finally, I believe that the most important and valuable thing I have done with my class is establishing strong working relationships. I have taken time to get to know my children well and will always celebrate personal successes and effort, rather than simply children's best end-products. Rewarding and praising children individually and recognising how hard they've worked to achieve something boosts children's confidence and willingness to take risks, as well as strengthening your relationships with your children.

Emily Godding, Primary ECT

Key takeaways

- Knowing your pupils, particularly their strengths, is key to being able to meet their needs.

- Drawing on a range of quality-first teaching strategies, such as modelling, flexible grouping, providing practical and visual resources and ensuring that there is a clear learning objective and success criteria, benefits all pupils.

- Every child with an identified SEND need has different needs.

- Our role in school is not to diagnose but to support the needs of the pupils that we have in our class.

- You need a range of strategies to support pupils in order to find what works most effectively for them.

CHAPTER 9

PUPIL

FEEDBACK

 Daily tip

Mr T's NQT/ECT support
@MrTs_NQTs

Live marking! In maths particularly, when you or your TA are circulating around the children, mark as you go. It provides instant feedback to children, can help you to identify common misconceptions and saves you time marking them later.

In this chapter we will:

➡️ Explore what effective feedback looks like.

➡️ Identify ways to provide feedback to pupils.

Feedback has frequently been identified as one of the top teaching and learning strategies that has the biggest impact on pupils for the lowest cost to schools. Getting it right, however, is not always easy.

I have spent years providing feedback to pupils, ECTs and experienced teachers with the view to help them to identify strengths and to improve. In this chapter, we are focusing on feedback to pupils, but some of the strategies that I have learned from working with ECTs and experienced teachers have influenced the way in which I deliver feedback to pupils.

Effective feedback

Whoever the feedback is aimed at, the purpose should always be about helping pupils to identify what they have done well and why, and what they need to improve next and how. So let's break it down!

■ Content

The content of your feedback may be dictated by your school's feedback policy, but for me it is important to make time to celebrate the strengths as well as the areas for development. I once worked with a school that only provided feedback focused on areas for development, without providing positive feedback identifying strengths. This was a few years ago and things may have changed, but their argument was that pupils only focused on areas to improve. However, for me, positive feedback and identifying strengths have two clear benefits. The first is that pupils need to know what they have done well in order to experience success. There may be many pupils in the class who only hear negative language at home and from others. That positive feedback and the chance to have something celebrated may help children to find confidence in and a love for a subject, or to find confidence in themselves. The second is that sometimes pupils don't know what they are doing well and why it is good – and anyone who is learning something new may not fully comprehend these concepts. Providing feedback highlighting their strengths will reinforce and help them to recognise what is going well.

After highlighting the positives, move onto the next steps. Many schools will use a system where there should be more positive feedback than next steps so that targets are clear and actionable – for example, two stars and a wish. Pupils must be able to understand what is expected of them and their next steps should be achievable. For some pupils, we can consider where they need to be in relation to age-related objectives, and whether they will be able to meet them comfortably. However, other pupils may need much smaller, more precise steps, in order to allow them to experience success and make progress towards larger goals. Considering this when setting targets/next steps in your feedback is important.

The other key thing to remember is that any feedback you provide during learning should be related to the learning objective and the success criteria. Imagine as a trainee being told that to be successful you need to do X, Y and Z and then being given feedback where you are told that you need to improve G! It would be confusing. This is the same for pupils. If you show that the learning intention for the lesson and the success criteria are the most important elements, through focusing your feedback on these areas, it will mean that pupils value them too.

◼ Timeliness

When is the best time to provide feedback to pupils? For me, it is during the learning rather than after it. Let me explain. Providing feedback during the learning can help students to avoid cementing misconceptions and will allow them time to implement their feedback straight away. Also, if pupils are involved in writing an extended piece over a few days, or completing a project over a number of lessons, providing feedback during the process will have the greatest impact. I always felt that providing pupils with extensive feedback after a piece of work was completed would have a limited impact. It would mean pupils recalling this for the next piece of work that they completed (which could be a different project or style of writing). The impact of the feedback coming at the end will be much less than the feedback provided during the learning, where pupils can have the opportunity to act on it immediately.

◼ Impact

What impact does your feedback have? So often I hear and see teachers providing high-quality feedback, but the impact is limited. When next steps are provided for pupils, it is important that they know what that feedback looks like in practice, but also that they receive support and time to develop those next steps. If you provide feedback to pupils, ensure that they have time to act on it. This could be straight away, in the next session or in between lessons. Time to act on feedback is vital for its impact. Moreover, it is important that support or interventions are put in place for pupils. If you find that you have provided the same next step for a pupil that you have provided on a previous occasion, it could be that specific support or intervention is needed. For example, when teaching in Key Stage 1, I often found myself asking students to use capital letters or full stops more accurately (or at all). However, I never spent time teaching them how they should be used, and then wondered why they were not able to achieve the next step. So I made sure that when pupils found it difficult to achieve their next steps, I put an intervention in place or made a focused teaching group in lessons to support pupils in developing their understanding of what their next step in learning would be.

COACHING MOMENT

▶ Do you always provide positive feedback to pupils and identify strengths?

▶ How do you ensure that next steps can be achieved by pupils?

▶ When do pupils get the opportunity to act on the feedback that they are given?

▶ How often do you provide the same 'next steps' feedback for pupils and not see an improvement? How could you support this?

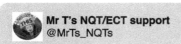

Mr T's NQT/ECT support
@MrTs_NQTs

Daily tip

Choose the timing of your feedback (written or verbal) carefully. Make sure that the children will have the opportunity to act on the feedback that they are given. Feedback on a finished piece of work can be pointless. Feedback during the learning has a far greater impact.

Strategies for feedback

The advice in this section comes with the awareness that there will be schools that have clear marking and feedback policies to which you will have to adhere. I have worked in schools where every child had to have written feedback in their books during every lesson; in a school where verbal feedback was expected and limited written feedback provided; and in a school where strengths were identified in one colour, areas for development in another and the children's responses in a third.

The school's marking policy will outline the ways in which you should feed back to pupils and how frequently this should be done. For example, a school I worked in identified that all work needed to be acknowledged, but 50 per cent should be marked in detail each week, with areas of strength and development being identified in relation to the learning objective and success criteria. There were symbols that were used for younger pupils to identify key features, such as punctuation and use of adjectives. A similar letter code was developed for older pupils along with written feedback. Verbal feedback could also be captured through the letters VF in pupils' work, in order to capture the impact of verbal feedback. How has the work improved after the feedback? However, many schools are now looking to move away from written feedback and to move towards verbal and/or whole-class feedback.

Whatever your school's marking policy, there are strategies that you can employ to ensure that feedback is timely and effective.

■ Live marking

… or marking in the lesson! This is something that I have said so often in observations of ECTs and trainees. They are busy going around to pupils, providing great verbal feedback and then moving on to support the next pupil. As you are providing feedback, use those two minutes to mark the work – it provides instant visual feedback for pupils and saves you time after the lesson.

■ Peer-/self-marking

Involving pupils in marking their own and others' work can really help them to reflect on their own development and identify their strengths and next steps. I have done this in a variety of ways.

Utilising clear, specific success criteria

Having success criteria that pupils know and understand can make peer-/self-marking really effective. It is important that pupils know what the success criteria look like so that they can identify them in their own and others' work. For example, for younger pupils, during handwriting practice, success criteria may be as simple as: 'letters sitting on the line' and 'clear ascenders and descenders' – pupils will be easily able to spot these in their work. For older pupils, it can be more complex, such as: 'speech correctly punctuated', 'use of simple and complex sentences' and 'relative clauses used to add detail' – still precise and easy for children to identify, but the skills required are much more complex.

Using marking sheets/check sheets

This involves providing pupils with the correct answers/prompt sheets to check their work against. These can be put on the wall and covered with a piece of coloured paper, and pupils can be directed to them when they have completed their work. This does not allow pupils to understand where they have gone wrong, but it does save you time on marking, and helps pupils to know which areas they need to review again.

Remember that peer- and self-assessment can be a hugely valuable way for pupils to engage with their own reflection on their work, if they are guided correctly.

■ Whole-class feedback

This is something that you will be doing frequently, but sometimes it is important to formalise and recognise the effective strategies that you are using. When the majority of pupils have made an error or displayed a misconception, whole-class feedback can be a great way in which to address it. This can involve using plenaries or mini plenaries (see Chapter 11), or starting the next lesson by sharing examples of the error/misconception and then providing pupils with the correct understanding, followed by time to address it. For example, if pupils are incorrectly punctuating speech by missing out the punctuation before closing the speech, share an example from a pupil's book or your own creation, identifying why it is wrong. Keep the focus on where the punctuation should go, showing the pupils how it should look and giving one or two correct examples to model the correct way to punctuate. Finally, provide the pupils with a set amount of time to review their own writing to make the corrections.

This can be a great way to reduce the marking needed for a common misconception. It also means that misconceptions can be addressed before they become embedded.

■ Whole-class feedback sheets

As many schools move away from individually written feedback, whole-class feedback/marking sheets are often used to capture the information about pupils' performance in a lesson. This involves identifying pupils who have exceeded the learning or who may need additional support, and identifying key errors and misconceptions that can feed into whole-class feedback during the next session. This is not something that you can do instead of following your school's marking and feedback policy, but it could be worth considering the prompts that would be captured on the following sheet to help you to adapt your teaching in future sessions.

Here is an example of a whole-class feedback/marking sheet. Please note, this should not be done on top of marking pupils' work!

Lesson:	Date:
Learning objective:	Success criteria:
Common errors/misconceptions:	Next steps for all pupils:
How the errors/misconceptions will be addressed:	Pupils who may need further support:
Pupils who need further challenge:	What support is needed:
Considerations for teaching this lesson again:	When the support will be delivered/by whom:

COACHING MOMENT

▶ What does your school's marking policy suggest about the frequency and structure of feedback and marking?

▶ How many ways do you provide feedback to pupils?

▶ What feedback systems do you find most effective for pupils?

Mr T's NQT/ECT support
@MrTs_NQTs

Daily tip

When using peer marking, utilise really strict criteria to begin with. E.g. highlight the best adjective or underline where there is a missing full stop. This can help you with marking, and also help to focus the children without them going crazy with the highlighter!

Thoughts from an ECT

When I started my ECT year, I felt quite overwhelmed by the prospect of having a full set of English and maths books to mark every day on top of all of my other work. My training year had been fully on placement and so I had always shared marking with my mentor – not to mention the COVID lockdown meaning that I'd never experienced being solely responsible for marking a whole class set of books. For the first few weeks, I quite enjoyed sitting and writing feedback in each child's book, only to realise that they never read my personal comments and, more importantly, they weren't responding to them. I spoke to some colleagues and realised that they were giving feedback in a much more constructive and much less time-consuming way.

I put my newfound knowledge into practice the next day – going forward, I would only look at a handful of English books from each lesson and would not sit and write the same thing in each maths book. By changing my feedback to 'whole class', where I would identify common mistakes and share them on my board in the following lesson to reteach or clarify the misunderstanding, I was able to cut my marking time down significantly. More importantly, pupils were listening to the feedback and improving their work going forward, because their errors and misconceptions were being corrected as opposed to just written about in their books. My feedback was becoming much more meaningful, as it was directly impacting the pupils' work and understanding.

Similarly, my maths feedback needed to be streamlined. I changed my method, no longer writing in every book and being ignored, but instead keeping a quick check of which children had grasped the learning and which hadn't, but more importantly I was making a note of common errors and reteaching them the next day. My previous feedback was a waste of my time – the pupils were not reflecting on it or learning anything from it, and I wasn't keeping an accurate record of their achievements, other than in their books. Now I have a very simple tick sheet to record the children's understanding of each objective and a notebook to record regular errors or misconceptions that need to be picked up. Again, the pupils learn from the feedback and I feel that I have a better understanding of their abilities and achievements.

Any feedback that I give to my pupils now follows this format – reteaching mistakes.

Overall, I started my teaching career with a preconceived idea of what marking and feedback needed to look like, but I have quickly learned that feedback needs to be effective. I am very lucky to work in a school that understands the benefits of – and encourages the use of – whole-class feedback. Effective feedback is one of my most important teaching tools.

Hannah Smith, Primary ECT

Key takeaways

- Know your school's marking/feedback policy.
- Be clear about the purpose of the feedback that you are providing to pupils.
- Ensure that feedback is always impactful and achievable for the pupils.
- Utilise a variety of strategies to provide feedback to pupils in order to make the biggest impact possible.
- Ensure that time is provided for pupils to respond to feedback and support is provided for pupils who need it in order to achieve those next steps.

CHAPTER 10
DATA AND
ASSESSMENT

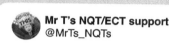  **Daily tip**

Mr T's NQT/ECT support
@MrTs_NQTs

When your school is asking for data to be provided, make sure you spend the time considering each pupil. When identifying if pupils have achieved an objective or not, if I can say yes straight away, I always go with it. If I have to stop and think, chances are they are not yet secure!

In this chapter we will:

➡ Look at day-to-day data and assessments and how they can be used effectively.

➡ Consider how data can be used to support you with pupil progress meetings.

➡ Identify the expectations if you are working with a year group involved in statutory assessments.

Data and assessment are not often the parts of the job that excite and enthuse us. However, they are important parts of being a teacher and allow us to identify strengths and next steps for pupils. Having held the role of assessment lead, I have had to make data and assessments work for the pupils and staff in my school. I have spent many an hour tweaking and developing Excel spreadsheets and looking at data to identify strengths for the school. (I actually quite enjoyed it – sad, I know.)

Class data – or should that be information?

When we think of data, we think of numerical information that can be 'crunched' and used to identify trends. But on a day-to-day basis, the 'data' that you gather will be more qualitative. It will be through those observations that you make, the questions that you ask and the marking that you do.

Assessment can be categorised into either formative assessment – information that *informs* the next steps, or summative assessment – information that *sums* up a pupil's journey and shows where they are at that moment in time. In my opinion, very few assessments are ever truly summative. Every assessment that we do can inform future teaching and next steps for pupils.

■ Learning objectives and success criteria

There is an overlap here with the curriculum and planning chapter. But to make assessment effective, it is important that both we and pupils understand what they are being assessed against. I have spent a long time refining the purpose and structure of the learning objectives and the success criteria that I use (see Chapter 7), but the most important thing is that both you and the pupils know what it is you want them to gain from the lesson, and that they – and you – know what this looks like.

There are a few key assessment strategies that I have found to be effective at helping me to get a greater insight into where pupils are and what their next steps should be.

■ Observations

We touched on this in Chapter 8, but observations are a great way of gathering an understanding of *how* pupils are working. Through observing pupils working, we can see the processes that they are undertaking, helping us to identify how they tackle their learning and allowing us to identify misconceptions. Having worked in EYFS for a couple of years, where observation was the main way of assessing pupils, I discovered that when I did observe, I needed to approach from two perspectives: having the focus of the lesson in mind – the intended success criteria and learning outcome for the lesson – and also being open to seeing what else the pupil was showing me. For example, in maths, the focus may be on addition. However, through observations I would also be able to tell a pupil's ability to recognise and form numbers correctly, and whether they could count accurately with one-to-one correspondence, in addition to their ability to add. As an EYFS practitioner, observations will be your bread and butter each day. However, in other year groups there may be specific subjects for which observations can be more planned and scheduled, such as PE. Whilst you will be observing informally all the time during PE, there may be key windows at the end of a unit of work in which you may wish to carry out formal observations. Equally, observations can be used whenever you want to gather additional information about a pupil or a subject. You can schedule these yourself, or there may be windows, such as EHCP reviews (Chapter 5), where these opportunities for observation will be dictated by the SLT.

■ Knowledge checks

By knowledge checks, I mean things that pupils just need to know – things like spellings, word/sound recognition, number bonds, times tables and so on. These may be dictated by your school and set as 'non-negotiables', which all pupils should know by the end of the year. You can also create your own non-negotiables based on the knowledge that pupils need identified in the National Curriculum. These can be a great way in which to identify gaps that may impact pupils' progress. For example, if a pupil cannot recognise the digraph 'ai', we cannot expect them to be able to blend words containing that sound. However, so often I see in schools endless spelling and times table tests being undertaken and pupils being stuck making the same mistakes week in, week out. Spelling tests are a particular bugbear of mine when they are not used effectively and have no impact on pupils! The pupils in the class who struggle with their spelling can often be sent home with lists of words to practise, only to come to school to score 0 on the spelling test and then be given a new list of words that they then won't/can't learn, only to fail again the following week. It is vital that the knowledge that we gain from these skills checks makes an impact on what *we* do as teachers. At my school, we shifted our focus; instead of sending words home, we started an intervention for those pupils who needed additional support with spelling. My TA would work with them for ten minutes after lunch each day, focusing on practising the spellings, looking at root words and so on. We also moved to a bespoke way of assessing spelling; we created word lists that were progressive. Pupils worked their way through the lists so that they were working at an appropriate level – for example, we would not have sent home '-ed' ending words to pupils who were still struggling to spell 'of' and 'was' correctly. This made a hugely positive impact. Pupils experienced success, which we know then drives intrinsic motivation.

■ Hot and cold tasks

Hot tasks, or exit tickets, can be a great way in which to quickly judge, at the end of a lesson or sequence of learning, where pupils are and to help you to inform next steps. It is a simple task that shows how much the pupils have grasped the content being taught. In EYFS, it could be as simple as 'show me 4'. Pupils could draw or photograph an example of '4'. For a more complex concept, it could be: Tick the equation that would have a negative number as an answer:

1. $5 + -7 =$
2. $7 - 5 =$
3. $5 - -7 =$

These equations could also be used as a 'cold' task at the start of the lesson and a 'hot' task at the end, to help you to assess pupils' understanding before and after learning.

Make sure that the task is quick, simple and allows for you to quickly identify pupils' understanding (we don't want to add excessively to your marking workload).

You can then use the outcome of the hot task to adapt your groups for the next day (see Chapter 8).

There are other class-based strategies that we can use for assessment, such as peer- and self-assessment and live marking – more detail on these can be found in Chapter 9.

COACHING MOMENT

▶ How often do you observe your pupils? What might you be able to find out about them?

▶ What assessment opportunities/systems do you have in your class? What information do they provide you with?

▶ How do you know at the end of the lesson how successful pupils have been?

Mr T's NQT/ECT support
@MrTs_NQTs

Daily tip

Every type of assessment will tell you something about a child's next steps. Make sure that you use what your assessment tells you, otherwise it becomes a box-ticking exercise and has no impact on pupil progress.

♡   ⟳   ♡   ⬆

What happens with my data?

Every school is different now in the way in which it tracks and monitors pupils' progress. Pre-2014, all schools used a common language of levels. However, this disappeared with the new curriculum, and the idea of being at 'age-related expectations' became the focus, with some pupils working towards and others working at greater depth.

This presented schools with the challenge of deciding how best to track, monitor and assess pupils' progress against the National Curriculum. Eight years on and the dust has settled and, with Ofsted's focus on internal data shifting away from trawling through data with a fine-tooth comb, schools are now in the position where their internal tracking should be focused on pupil progress, as opposed to being a tool used to justify performance to external bodies.

Each school has its own internal tracking system, and your school will provide you with support and training in how it works and when you will be expected to complete data input (usually once per term). After you have lovingly spent time inputting data into your school's tracking system – which should not be an onerous task and should have a clear relevance to your teaching and your pupils – what happens next will vary from school to school.

In my school, teachers were asked to identify where pupils were in relation to key objectives taken from the National Curriculum for the core subjects – reading, writing and maths (RWM). This then highlighted which objectives pupils were secure with, which objectives needed a greater focus for all pupils and which objectives a small group of pupils may benefit from a focused intervention to achieve – all with the aim that we were working towards pupils working at age-related expectations. I always wanted to ensure that data was purposeful for teachers and pupils. I am not a believer in gathering data for the sake of it.

If you are asked for data that does not feel purposeful and that you don't feel will make an impact on the progress of your pupils, speak to your mentor. You may not be able to change the process, but having a conversation with your mentor may help you to understand its purpose, or even encourage them to consider the effectiveness of the data that you are being asked to provide. So often in schools things happen because 'we've always done it that way'. As a fresh pair of eyes, you may be able to help the school reflect on this.

From a leadership point of view, the data provided is then fed into a bigger system that would allow me to monitor specific groups of pupils across the school, and it also helps to drive the focus of pupil progress meetings.

Pupil progress meetings allow for the SLT to establish the story behind the numbers, to identify what is happening with pupils and what further support may be needed. The chances are that pupil progress meetings will take place between you and a member of the SLT – depending on the size of the school, it could be the head, the phase lead or the head of year/department.

When ECTs experience their first pupil progress meeting, there can be a huge trepidation about what to expect. In my mind, whenever leading these it was about celebrating what the ECT had done to help the pupils to achieve and the support and guidance that they had provided for those pupils who were not achieving as well. This is where data gives only half a picture. It does not account for a family bereavement, a change in the circumstances at home or the fact that a pupil may be struggling with their mental health at that moment in time. In a small school, every member of the SLT will be aware of these issues, but in any school, you are the one teaching the pupils day in and day out, and you will hold the deepest source of knowledge about those children.

These are the questions that are likely to be asked during pupil progress meetings:

> I can see that the pupils are making great progress in… What do you feel is helping them to achieve this?

> This pupil has made great progress in… What have you done to help them to get there?

> This group of pupils appears to not be making as much progress as other pupils. What support can we offer? What have you tried already?

> This is a pupil who has been at age-related expectations in previous years; has something happened?

It is not about catching you out, but teaching comes with a level of accountability, and the SLT have a duty to ask questions to help you to reflect and to support you if needed.

To help you to prepare for your pupil progress meetings, it is always worth spending time going through the data system. The chances are that you will be able to spot the pupils who you will be asked about. It can help you to feel confident in preparing. I always used to provide time for my NQTs/ECTs to look through their class data with me during their non-contact time. This helped them to get the most from the data system, as well as helping them to feel confident going into their pupil progress meetings.

Don't be afraid to take pupils' work with you to share and celebrate, or to show where pupils are finding things challenging and the support that you are putting in place.

COACHING MOMENT

- ▶ How does your school monitor pupil progress?
- ▶ How much do you engage with your school's data-tracking system?
- ▶ How will the data support you in your teaching?
- ▶ Which pupils have made great progress? Which do you need more support with?

Mr T's NQT/ECT support
@MrTs_NQTs

Daily tip

Formative assessment is your greatest weapon in securing the progress of pupils. Using questions, live marking, clear objectives and peer- and self-assessment can give you a great understanding of where pupils are in their learning!

Statutory assessment

Statutory assessments are those that pupils undertake at key points in their academic career. They are a type of summative assessment that capture a pupil's achievement at that moment in time in a specific subject or area. I taught in Year 2 in my NQT year and was very quickly introduced to the idea of statutory assessment and how important these measures are to schools and parents – less so to pupils at that point in time. At the time when I administered Statutory Assessment Tasks (SATs) at the end of Key Stage 1, the aim was to get pupils to a Level 2! This data was then tracked and used to judge the effectiveness of the school to see whether by the time they reached the end of Key Stage 2 they were achieving a Level 4 – satisfactory progress. This always felt like a bit of a damning judgement for those pupils, as for some this was a huge achievement. Looking forward to now, new statutory assessments exist in primary and have been tweaked in secondary.

At the time of writing, these are the current statutory assessment points that exist in mainstream education in England. For those in other countries, it is worth looking at the government website for further details.

Task	Year group administered
Reception baseline assessment	Within the first six weeks of pupils starting in Reception
Early Years Foundation Stage Profile	Reception (June)
Phonics screening check	Year 1 (June)
End of Key Stage 1 SATs	Year 2 (May/June)
Multiplication times tables check	Year 4 (June)
End of Key Stage 2 SATs	Year 6 (May)
GCSEs	Year 11 or earlier (May/June)
A levels	Year 13 or earlier (May/June)

As you can see from the table above, there are now only two year groups in primary that are not involved in any form of statutory assessment.

The purpose and content of each of these assessments varies, but below we will look at your involvement in each of these.

Whichever statutory assessment you find yourself involved with (and it will no doubt happen at some point in your career), it is important that you are familiar with the assessment and reporting arrangements (ARA) for the tasks administered. The ARA outlines the expectations for schools in relation to the statutory assessment being delivered, from the timescales of when tests should be administered to details of data that will need to be reported and by when. If you pop ARA and the subject into your favourite search engine, it will get you to the right place. For GCSE, ensure that you are familiar with the exam board expectations – seek support from your head of department.

As an ECT, part of your involvement with assessments will be using the ARA (with support from your SLT) to ensure that processes are followed and that you know what is expected of you. My NQT year was in Year 2, so I was thrown into SATs early on in my career. I worked alongside a more experienced teacher in Year 2, so was well supported. I have always wanted any ECT to feel confident if they are in a year with statutory assessment, and the following areas are some of the things that will support you (or questions to ask or things to find out) if you find yourself in a year group with statutory assessment.

■ How are pupils assessed?

The assessment of pupils varies depending on the statutory assessment that is being undertaken. Some are tests that must be administered at a specific point in time; others require you to gather evidence over time to make informed teacher assessments against the given criteria. Ultimately, the ARA is the bible for this, but your SLT will be able to guide you on what this should look like and offer you support.

If you have to gather evidence, this could be through pupils' coursework or through systems that your school suggests – monthly writing or end-of-unit tests, for example. However, there will always be guidance about what evidence you are looking for. An example of this is found at the end of Key Stage 1 and 2, where teacher assessment frameworks are used to support teachers in their teacher assessments (STA, 2018).

Regardless of whether you are collating coursework for A levels or evidence of writing for Key Stage 1, it is important that you use the guidance from the DfE or the relevant exam board to ensure that you are collecting the right evidence and that it shows what you need it to. You will receive support from the SLT and your mentor on this, so you will not have to shoulder the burden alone.

If there are timed/formal tests that need to be administered as part of the assessment, then the ARA or exam board will provide specific guidance for this. As an ECT in secondary or further education, you would not be expected to invigilate an exam, but you may be asked to support during mock exams. This can be good experience and help you to understand and better prepare your pupils for what they should expect. (However, it should be in lieu of teaching your class and not as an addition.)

In primary education, tests are usually administered by you, the class teacher, with support from the SLT. This is important for younger pupils, as it provides them with the security of working with a familiar face. There are always specific windows for when tests must be administered and guidance on how they should be done. Most require you to open materials on the day of the test and then store any materials securely until a specific date, to avoid malpractice. Again, this is not something that you would have to shoulder alone; your SLT will support you with the administration of any tests.

■ Reporting grades

Teacher assessment is an important part of most statutory assessment, whether it is to inform the potential outcomes for pupils or to specify the final grade that is provided to pupils and parents. How grades are reported will be defined in the ARA, but you may be asked to provide your evidence and judgement to the SLT, or you may find yourself in the position of working with a member of the SLT to input data to return to the local authority and the DfE. This was always one of those 'read the grade, type it and then check it again' moments. This will only be the case for internally marked and assessed assessments; anything externally marked will be pre-populated, but you may need to add teacher assessments to the grades.

As an ECT in your first year working in Reception, Year 2 or Year 6, you will be subject to external moderation by the local authority. You will be invited to a moderation clinic, where the process will be outlined. The focus will be on using the Early Learning Goals (ELGs) or teacher assessment framework for some randomly selected pupils and giving you the opportunity to share your evidence for the pupils. Your judgements for these pupils will be validated by the moderator. (In most cases, judgements are maintained, but if they are changed it is normally for the better – as teachers, we can often err on the side of caution!) The moderator who arrives will usually be someone who works in the year group that they are moderating and will have been trained by the local authority in the expected process. They will absolutely understand what it is like for you in your position, and will offer advice and support. A member of the SLT will usually be with you as well for the moderation process.

COACHING MOMENT

- ▶ If you are involved in a year with statutory assessment, are you clear about what this looks like?

- ▶ What support are you receiving to be able to administer the tasks accurately?

- ▶ Have you read the assessment and reporting arrangements (ARA) published by the DfE for the assessment tasks that you need to administer?

Thoughts from an ECT

One could argue that teaching in Year 5 is rather fortunate, as it's one of only two years in primary education where there is no external formal assessment. However, there is so much more to assessment than the noise in the media. As I reflect on my first two terms of teaching, I've realised that assessment, particularly formative, plays an important role in my day-to-day work.

Data-gathering is important; as teachers, we get a feel for our pupils' attainment but we need quantitative data to back up the 'feels'. In my school, we test formatively at the beginning of each module (apart from English and reading). This provides a clear comparison of progress throughout the module. We give the same multiple-choice test at the end of the module, albeit we add a tell-me-more question for further challenge. At a class level it provides you with information to reflect on your teaching: Are there trends in the summative assessment? Did most of the class not get a certain aspect of the topic? At an individual level it shows progress and can be a catalyst for small-group work to clarify teaching points. As a new teacher, I find this data immensely helpful, both for self-reflection and for lesson planning.

In terms of assessment, individual whiteboards (IWBs) are your friends. You can ask 30 children the same question at the same time and it can be very revealing. What they write is important but there are other assessment clues. Are they scribbling away confidently and quickly? Is there copying going on? Does it reveal misconceptions or is it just a spelling mistake? Have any of the answers surprised you and if so, why? I could write many more questions, but if the children hadn't used a whiteboard, how else would these questions have arisen? Have rules, though; whiteboards can be used for doodling too. If you think that the information they are writing down is worth coming back to, pop it in a notebook.

Marking can take an age and you will need to follow your school's policy. However, live marking, especially in maths, is extremely useful. Get the TA to do it too, as it flags up misconceptions prior to the end of the lesson. You can be considering your next lesson before you've even finished the one that you're teaching. It can be an indication to stop and change the focus; abandoning your lesson plan is not a bad thing if you are responding to your assessment findings.

In English, I find pupil conferencing helpful – I'll annotate their margin with a 'VF' (verbal feedback). I've also tried to include whole-class feedback in the introduction to the lesson; it frames why I'm focusing on certain areas and it will be something that I want pupils to focus on when they are editing their work. Which brings me to pupil assessment. This can be incredibly powerful: children will look differently at the work of others. Checking your own work is difficult; even as adults we read what we think we have written, yet a child can learn a lot from reading the work of another. Again, have guidelines – from the basics of pen colour, so it's clear to see the author, the pupil assessor and your annotations. Also, how do they word their feedback? Two stars and a wish works well in primary.

Eventually, though, summative and, at times, statutory assessment occurs. For the majority, the results shouldn't be a surprise as you've been informally assessing as you go. However, there will be anomalies. Help pupils to prepare by providing questions in the format that the assessment will take – for example, if your school uses computer-based multiple-choice testing and statutory assessment is written, the pupils will need practice at framing their answers. Also encourage good test behaviour in the classroom; this may be showing workings clearly (this can be an area where IWBs need to be used with care), writing complete answers or even just working in silence for a set period.

One last note: the clearer that you are with your assessment, the easier it is to explain and justify to your SLT and parents. As a general principle, data should be gathered once and used many times – you should be able to justify your assessments and provide suggestions as to how the child can progress. In general, no one – not you, the teacher, the pupil, the parent or the SLT – should be surprised by end-of-year results. Your assessment throughout the year will inform and communicate.

Louise Grant, Primary ECT

Key takeaways

- Most assessment that you undertake is informal but provides a wealth of information.

- Make sure that every assessment you undertake informs what you do for pupils.

- Don't fear pupil progress meetings; view them as a chance to celebrate what you do and what the pupils have achieved.

- If you are working in a year with statutory assessment, it is important that you know the expectations for their administration.

- If you are selected for moderation, it is a supportive process and it is about sharing your evidence and the reason for your judgements.

CHAPTER 11
DEVELOPING PEDAGOGY

 Mr T's NQT/ECT support
@MrTs_NQTs

Daily tip

Convince me...

One of the most powerful questions you can ask is: Convince me that four is the answer, or convince me why you chose that adverb. Encourage children to ask each other using the question stem. It gives even more opportunity to develop reasoning and understanding.

In this chapter we will:

→ Explore a range of approaches that will support and guide you with continuing development in your teaching.

→ Look at how you can make the best decision about which strategies are most appropriate to use for your class, subject and the content that you are teaching.

Pedagogy is one of those words that only has relevance in teaching. For me, it is about the way in which you choose to teach pupils: what techniques and strategies you are using to facilitate learning in your class. This chapter will be about the strategies that I have found to be most effective but also the ones that ECTs often find challenging or that I often find myself guiding ECTs towards using to support them in developing their teaching.

Modelling

We have touched on modelling in a few of the other chapters, but it is one of those key practices that should be part of your toolkit and utilised in every lesson. I have sat in many observed lessons where the pupils are sent away to work and are not clear about what is expected of them, because the task and/ or expectations have not been visually modelled.

Seven years into my teaching career, I had the chance to visit another school as part of an Assessment for Learning project. I was blown away by the way in which the class teacher utilised a visualiser to model the activity to pupils, as well as to share where pupils had demonstrated the expected learning objective and success criteria (see Chapter 7 and the mini plenary section below). I rushed back to my school and managed to negotiate funding with my headteacher for all classes to have a visualiser. Fifteen years on, and visualisers are now commonplace in most classes (tablets can also be used to achieve the same result). What a visualiser allows you to do is live-model exactly what you expect the pupils to do. I have used it to model the correct layout for how a piece of work should be presented, and to show how you can use manipulatives in mathematics to solve problems. When carrying out a piece of shared writing with pupils, the opportunities that it creates are incredible. I am conscious that not every classroom may have access to a visualiser, but if you get the opportunity to request equipment, it is the one thing that you should ask for.

Of course, you can model the expectations in other ways, such as using your interactive whiteboard to show an image of the activity to be completed, or using a flip chart or sugar paper to model the activity. By utilising effective modelling, it removes confusion for pupils about expectations and allows you to pause and demonstrate the thinking processes behind each step that you are taking, as well as to address misconceptions along the way (see the section on misconceptions below).

Live modelling can be an area that ECTs and experienced teachers shy away from. Often ECTs worry about live modelling and are concerned that pupils may want them to use a word that they can't spell or that they might make a mistake. In actual fact, when these opportunities arise, it is beneficial for pupils to see you model the strategies that you advise them to use. For example, if they do suggest a word that you aren't sure how to spell during a piece of modelled writing, use the strategies that you teach the children: modelling dictionary skills, or using phonetic/spelling patterns. Similarly, if you make a mistake in a maths problem, by modelling through the strategy, you can work back and identify where the mistake has been made and then model the process of correcting it. These are all key learning moments for the pupils, and by you modelling the processes, it will reaffirm and reassure them.

As part of the modelling process and to support pupils, a WAGOLL (What A Good One Looks Like) can be a great way of demonstrating expectations, allowing for pupils to establish and discover the features for themselves. I have found that having a WABOLL (What A Bad One Looks Like) can provide a good comparator and support pupils in spotting what makes a good piece of work because of how it is better than the bad one. There will be lots of WAGOLLs out there that you can use, but keeping work from previous year groups as an example can be great. Always avoid using examples from the current class – especially for WABOLLs. Using anonymous examples allows the work to be 'dissected' without fear of personal offence.

Mr T's NQT/ECT support
@MrTs_NQTs

Daily tip

Never underestimate the power of live modelling. Using pre-made examples can help, but live modelling allows you to demonstrate the thought process and the 'how' and 'why' of what is being created. #YouGotThis

I do, we do, you do

Following on from modelling is the 'I do, we do, you do' approach. This strategy is something that I have found beneficial; it is hugely advocated by the mastery approach in mathematics but it also has transferability to other areas of the curriculum. The idea is that when new ideas or concepts are introduced, examples are modelled by the teacher (I do), then examples are worked through as a whole class or group, depending on the context (we do), and then pupils can work through examples independently (you do). The transition between the 'we do' and 'you do' section can be adapted as part of your teaching for different pupils. Utilising mini-whiteboards as a way of assessing how all pupils are doing with the content at the 'we do' stage allows you to know which pupils are ready for the independent 'you do' step, as well as to identify pupils who may benefit from further examples or more support.

This has always allowed me the opportunity to be able to flexibly group pupils or to direct the TA if needed to support specific groups or individuals.

Questioning

There is so frequently a discussion about whether teachers ask too many questions. I bet if you were to tally the number of questions that you asked in a lesson, you would probably hit nearly 100! As teachers, the majority of questions that we ask are to check or develop understanding. However, at times, we may focus on fact recall, rather than understanding, in the questions that we ask. But there is a place for this for some children. Let's unpick the type of questions that you may ask and the benefits of each.

■ Recall questions

These are the simple ones, like 'What is this part of the plant called?', 'What do we call the place where two edges meet?' and so on. They are there to check recall of knowledge – and, let's be clear, that is all they are. Although ascertaining whether or not pupils can remember something is important, it should not be the main reason why you are asking questions. For some pupils, though, it allows them to experience success. Some pupils may be reluctant to engage with questions during class discussions, so asking simple recall questions can build a sense of confidence and allow them to experience success.

■ Checking understanding questions

These are often the follow-up type of questions, or questions that require pupils to demonstrate a greater understanding than simple recall – for example, 'If I count in 4s, will I ever say the number 123?'. What we want is for pupils to demonstrate the understanding that when counting in 4s the numbers are always even, so the simple answer is 'no', but the follow-up would be 'How do you know?' or 'Convince me'. These questions allow you to check a level of understanding behind an answer. The example that I have used comes from maths, but this works in other subjects as well: 'Why have you used that exclamation mark there?', 'Why was the Roman invasion important for England?' and so on.

■ Deepening understanding questions

These are questions that allow pupils to apply their learning to a new context so that their learning becomes deeper. For example, let's build upon our counting in 4s question: 'So, if we know that when we count in 4s we will not say 123, what about if we were counting in 3s?' At this point, there may be an immediate 'yes' because the number ends in a 3, or a maybe, and pupils can then explore the answer. Again, this is a follow-up question, but it provides a deeper learning opportunity and a way in which to apply knowledge to a new situation. Examples from other subject areas include: 'What would happen to your character if you changed this adverb from silently to craftily?', 'Would we need to build a new castle in England?' and so on.

The checking understanding questions can be hugely useful for helping you to know whether pupils are ready to progress to the next steps in learning. Having pupils explain their understanding can help you to be certain that their learning is secure.

Now that we have considered the content of the questions, we also need to consider how we ask the questions.

So often I observe ECTs play question tennis with their classes – a question is thrown out to the pupils, a pupil responds, the teacher acknowledges, rephrases and then asks the next question, and we get this back and forth, like tennis. What we should be aiming for is something a bit more like basketball. The question is thrown out to the pupils and then it can be passed to other pupils before coming back to you as the teacher. By providing pupils with time to listen and respond to each other, you will get a wider sense of what pupils think and create a deeper level of understanding. We can do this by developing expectations where pupils can show whether they want to add a contribution to the discussion. You could use hands up, random selection or develop ways in which pupils can indicate whether they want to 'agree', 'build' or 'challenge'. I have seen schools where pupils use hand gestures – thumbs up for agree, crossed arms (*The X-Factor* style) for disagree/challenge and stacked hands to show that they want to build. Alternatively, pupils can be given cards or fans with symbols on that they can show when they want to contribute:

'Cold calling' can be another way to ensure the contributions of pupils in sessions. However, this needs to be preceded by plenty of thinking time or partner discussion time. Pupils who have poor working memories or cognition and learning concerns can find being put on the spot very stressful. By providing discussion and thinking time, we can address this and enable them to engage and experience success. For example, during paired talk time, I will work with specific pairs and ensure that they have developed answers. For some pupils I will even say that I will come to them first and that they have the time now to practise and rehearse their answer.

A great video of Dylan Wiliam – a guru for formative assessment and one of the authors of *Inside the Black Box* (Black and Wiliam, 1998) – talking about questioning, can be found on YouTube (2015).

Mini plenaries

In the days when I trained to teach, you had to have a plenary at the end of every lesson, and although thinking has moved on, mini plenaries are still such an important part of my teacher toolkit and something that I see so often would benefit trainees and ECTs. The reason for this is two-fold. Firstly, mini plenaries allow you to address common errors and misconceptions in learning, as well as to celebrate the way in which pupils are demonstrating the learning objective or success criteria. Secondly, they allow you a purposeful brain break for children. So often we expect children as young as five to write for extended periods of up to 30 minutes. For some 15-year-olds, this is a challenge! A mini plenary allows you to take control of lapses in concentration and provide something 'different' for your pupils to engage with before refocusing back on their task. Using a visualiser to share a good example or to make corrections, and then allowing pupils a couple of minutes to check their own or a peer's work before continuing, not only reinforces the expectations from the lesson but also allows pupils to regain purpose and focus before continuing with their task.

If I have had to answer the same question twice from pupils, I will also stop and use a mini plenary to address shared misconceptions, as the chances are that something in my explanation has not been effective and needs to be addressed.

A plenary is a chance to summarise the learning so far and allows pupils to reflect on their own position in response to this learning, and mini plenaries during the lesson can be much more purposeful at the time of the learning rather than at the end of the lesson (see Chapter 9 for further discussion of this area).

Daily tip

Mr T's NQT/ECT support
@MrTs_NQTs

Make use of mini plenaries to assess progress. Give children time to reflect on the success criteria and share good examples or how to improve. Use the opportunity to regroup the children to tackle any emerging needs.

I say, you say

This could also be called 'call and response' or 'choral chanting'. I have had the privilege of working in schools in quite deprived areas, where pupils' language and vocabulary skills have been very limited. During this time, I used a lot of 'I say, you say' to help pupils to develop vocabulary and understanding. For example, when introducing a new piece of vocabulary, the word would be said by you as a teacher, the pupils would then repeat the word after you, and then say it to the person sat next to them. I would repeat this twice, so that pupils had correctly said the word at least four times. After this, I would then introduce a simple accurate definition using the 'I say, you say' approach. For example, when introducing the word 'adverb', a simple definition would be 'a word that describes how something is being done' or 'a word that describes a verb'. Pupils would then have this 'hook' to support them. After the 'I say, you say' approach, I would then do a part of the chant. For example, I would say 'an adverb is…' and pupils would respond with 'a word that describes a verb', or I would say 'a word that describes a verb is called an…' and the pupils would respond with 'adverb'.

I have found this a really powerful way of helping pupils to learn vocabulary and develop an understanding of what words mean. This is an approach that works regardless of subject, and whilst I did use it to support pupils with limited vocabulary, it also helped those pupils who had a more developed vocabulary to secure new vocabulary more quickly.

Dual coding

Starting my teaching career in Key Stage 1 and EYFS, I spent so much time providing pupils with visual representations on which to help them 'hang' their learning. When providing instructions, I would frequently draw an image as I was talking it through, to support pupils in being able to recall the expectations for the tasks that they had to complete. For example, if pupils needed to write something, I would often draw a pencil writing on the board.

Later I started to do this when introducing new vocabulary. With each word, an image of that word would be presented. This then evolved into things like concept maps and story maps. All of this time I was utilising dual coding without consciously considering this. Dual coding is presenting pupils with information through two different channels: images and written words or images and spoken words. Dual coding is something that I did because it was good practice and I had found that it helped pupils to be able to discuss, retain and recall the concepts that were being discussed. We have all seen those brilliant videos where, as the presenter is talking, images are being drawn to represent what is being said. By activating two senses and creating greater connections between learning for pupils, they are more likely to acquire the knowledge and be more secure in its acquisition. So, when you are presenting complex ideas or introducing technical vocabulary, utilising dual coding can be a great way of securing them with pupils.

Misconceptions

I love a misconception. I find it fascinating how pupils develop their understanding of the world and how this is applied in new situations. For example, a child may learn the word 'pigeon' when they see a bird land in the garden. But then when a blackbird lands in a garden, it is also labelled a 'pigeon'. A misconception at its heart is a piece of knowledge or understanding that is incorrect or being applied incorrectly. One that springs to mind is a child writing 'one hundred and ten' as 1010. The first time that you teach a lesson or subject, there will be some misconceptions that you are aware of, but there will be new ones that appear that you can adapt and respond to through the use of mini plenaries. Every year you teach, you will add to your bank of potential misconceptions. These potential misconceptions can be used to shape your teaching, through modelling or utilising an example where the misconception is evident, so that it can be addressed by the whole class. I have always found that younger pupils, when working practically, can respond well to a puppet demonstrating a misconception for them to correct. For example, the puppet might spell a word wrongly or carry out a process in maths incorrectly. It avoids using another child to demonstrate the misconception and causing any increased anxiety for that child. Many maths mastery schemes will provide example misconceptions for pupils to address – for example, 'John says that if he has five coins, the total is 5p'. Again, these allow for misconceptions to be challenged without them being directed at a specific pupil.

Concept cartoons are another great way of dealing with misconceptions. They are often commonplace in maths and science (pop 'concept cartoons' into your preferred search engine). They provide examples of common misconceptions that can then be discussed and addressed before moving forwards. Once you get the hang of these, creating your own for those recurring misconceptions can be hugely beneficial.

Mr T's NQT/ECT support
@MrTs_NQTs

Utilise a puppet in maths! When planning a lesson, take time to consider the most common misconceptions children might have. Using a character or puppet can be a great way of demonstrating a misconception and addressing it without singling children out.

COACHING MOMENT

▶ Which approaches do you use already?

▶ Which do you think you would want to explore further and try in your own practice?

▶ Are there any that you would need to research further or find out more about?

Other approaches

There are myriad different teaching approaches out there, and this chapter has only scratched the surface. What is important is that you continue to try out and develop approaches that work for you, the content that you are teaching and the pupils with whom you are working. With support from your mentor, this is a time to take risks and try out new ways to develop approaches and learn from those that work well and from those that are less successful. You will continue to develop throughout your teaching career, and as a trainee or ECT you may have names like Vygotsky, Piaget and Bruner in your head; these people will inform some of the strategies that you use. Many of your strategies will evolve from the way in which your school chooses to teach, and others will develop from your own experience and what you find works for you and your pupils. There is value in all three of these approaches, but most important is that sense of an evolving picture. As I have mentioned previously, many of the approaches to learning that were advocated during my training have now come under scrutiny – accommodating for different learning preferences, for example. However, there are some things, such as modelling, that have remained constant, and developments in technology and our understanding mean that we can now model more effectively using visualisers, rather than having to photocopy onto transparencies to use on an overhead projector (there will be one gathering dust somewhere in your school).

Teaching strategies will develop over your teaching career. During my time, I have seen moments when visual, auditory and kinaesthetic opportunities have had to be planned in each lesson. I have also attended training about how to identify left- and right-brain learners and how it affects the way in which they learn. Most recently, there has been work exploring growth mindset, which has come under fire for its lack of empirical evidence. However, on the latter, pupils believing that they can improve and get better with effort can be no bad thing.

The point that I am making is that education shifts as our understanding of learning and child development develops and with the influence of educational policy. However, outlined in this chapter are the key approaches on which you will draw time after time in your own practice, and which will serve you well regardless of how the landscape of education changes.

COACHING MOMENT

▶ Which approaches suit you and your teaching style?

▶ When you are planning for your class, which approaches would suit the content that you are trying to teach?

▶ Which strategies would suit the pupils with whom you are working?

Thoughts from an ECT

Throughout our training year, pedagogy becomes a staple word within our vocabulary, and as a trainee in Wales it is something that is at the forefront of my teaching. To me, pedagogy is not only the way in which I teach my pupils but also encompasses the way in which I deliver those lessons. This is something that is constantly changing depending on what is happening within the school and what is happening within my class.

Fresh from training, you arrive at your new school bustling with ideas. You are excited to make your mark within your department and are eager to work with your pupils. What I have found, though, is that it took me a little while to adapt my pedagogical approaches to my classes because I didn't know the pupils well enough and they didn't know me. They were trying to work out what my style of teaching was too.

If I have a class that I know struggles with remembering certain facts or dates, we use random questions during the lesson. This works well during the lesson as it allows me to see what pupils know and whether there have been any misconceptions that I need to address before they leave the classroom. Questioning is a really effective tool for teachers, whether you use whiteboards, colour cards or hands up for the students.

For writing, I have found that modelling the work is one of the best tools that I can use. Using WAGOLLs (What A Good One Looks Like) allows your pupils to see exactly what you are expecting from their writing and how you would like them to set out their work. I usually tie this into 'I do, we do, you do' tasks, as this allows pupils to have the support to set out their writing before they write a sentence or paragraph by themselves. I will always put some typos within my work too, for the students to find, as we can then discuss the literacy side of their writing.

I think that the biggest thing I have found is not to panic or worry about whether you're ticking all of the boxes right away. It's hard, as you do compare yourself (no matter how many times you're told not to) to colleagues who seamlessly manage to do everything within a classroom without giving it much thought. However, you are new and still learning – and that's fine. Try new things, and if it doesn't work then reflect on why it didn't work. Maybe it was because the task was too hard for the needs of the pupils, or was it just that particular class that it didn't work with? Keep tweaking things, and magpie ideas from Twitter and from your colleagues.

Becky Roberts, Secondary history ECT

Key takeaways

- There are a vast range of pedagogical approaches out there to explore.

- Find the approaches that suit you, your pupils and the content being taught.

- Experimenting with different teaching strategies should be actively encouraged during your ECT years.

CHAPTER 12
WORKING WITH PARENTS AND CARERS

 Mr T's NQT/ECT support
@MrTs_NQTs

Parents of children with SEND hold the greatest amount of knowledge about their children. Utilising structured conversations is a great way of engaging parents and being able to work in partnership to support their child(ren). #YouGotThis

In this chapter we will:

➡️ Explore how to build effective relationships with parents through our day-to-day interactions.

➡️ Identify how to maximise parents' evenings and make these a positive experience for all.

➡️ Look at the purpose of reports and techniques for how to write them.

This chapter will outline the best ways to form positive working relationships with parents and carers in order to support the outcomes for pupils and consider effective ways to communicate with them. To aid with the flow of the chapter, the term 'parent' will be used to identify anyone with a caregiving responsibility for a child, whether that be a biological parent, grandparent, foster or adopted parent. What is most important for you to know is who the child's legal guardian is and who has parental responsibility. It may not always be their biological parent.

Working with parents can be the part of the job that causes you great anxiety – parents can be your greatest ally or your greatest antagonist. Sometimes the same parent can be both in the same meeting. We will look at the four key ways in which our interactions with parents can secure a productive relationship with them to ensure the best outcomes for the pupils: day-to-day interactions, parents' evenings, structured conversations and reports.

Day-to-day interactions

This is the bread and butter of your interactions with parents. It is the smiles as you walk through the playground through to the sponges that you are having thrown at you at PTA events.

As an established member of a school community, the pupils I taught knew what to expect before they even entered my classroom, because the parents spoke to each other. Every family I worked with created a connection with the community and led to establishing my place within it. This took time to develop but there are a few things that really helped me. (With a primary background myself, these will mostly focus on primary settings, but they can be transferred to secondary settings.)

> Smile and make eye contact: Much like when working with the pupils, having confidence in the way in which we act when we meet parents pays dividends. We want parents to know that when they leave their child in our care they can trust and have confidence in us.

> Find them before they find you: Stride with confidence up to the group of parents huddled in the corner to introduce yourself and make polite conversation. Building social capital is so important with parents; you want your first interactions to be focused on positives, establishing a professional and purposeful relationship. This then allows you to have those difficult conversations when needed.

> Get in there first: If an incident has happened during the school day, sometimes a phone call before pick-up or speaking to them before they have the chance to speak to their child can be a good way of showing that you are in control of the situation, you know what is going on and action has already been taken.

> Celebrate the positives: Whether you speak to them at the end of the day, send home postcards or telephone home, provide as much positive information about their child as possible. Some parents will have their own negative experiences of school and they may only have interactions with teachers that focus on where things have gone wrong. Be different: be the teacher that they feel is in their corner.

> Get stuck in: As the sponges to the face may have indicated, I often got all the best roles during PTA events! Being part of a school community means being part of the local community. As uncomfortable as it can be, speaking to parents in this setting allows you to continue to build professional relationships and allows them to see you as a human as much as a teacher.

> Protect yourself on social media: We have spoken about this previously, but it is really important. You are a human and have a life, but parents and pupils will try to find you on social media. Even if you work in Key Stage 1, you will still need to consider your pupils – I had a Year 1 child in my class with a very active Facebook account, so never assume! Your social media accounts need to be secure, and change your name if you haven't already. This does not fully protect you, but it does allow you to have a private life.

> Be honest: When you do need to have a difficult conversation with a parent, be honest about the event that happened and your understanding of it. Also be clear about the way forward – what will happen next. These conversations can be challenging and uncomfortable to think about, but once they have happened you can move forward from them.

> Apologise: If you make a mistake, own it! Never dig yourself into a deeper hole by lying about something that has happened. Apologise, acknowledge the mistake and establish a way to move forward.

> Disarm them: When an angry parent approaches you, striding across the playground (or over the phone), disarm them with a smile and by saying, 'Good morning Mr/Mrs X, isn't it a lovely morning/isn't the weather horrible this morning, how can I help?' The chances are that you will get a sarcastic response about it not being a particularly lovely morning, but it should start the ball rolling in a positive way.

> Offer them tea: Most disputes can be settled over a cup of tea and a biscuit. If you can get the class covered, or if you are at the end of the day, invite the parent in for a cup of tea and a biscuit. Parents ultimately want to be heard and to know that you are on the same page about their child and achieving the best for them.

> Know your tricky ones: Unless you are in EYFS, the chances are that someone else in the school has taught your pupils before. Find out which parents you need to make contact with early and which ones you need on side to make your life easier.

COACHING MOMENT

▶ How confident do you feel about approaching parents?

▶ How much contact will you have with parents? When would be the best time to speak to parents to start to develop a professional relationship?

▶ Who in your school is confident in speaking to parents? What techniques do they use?

▶ Which parents have already been identified to you?

▶ How secure/private is your social media? Do you need to curate the contents?

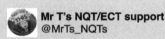

Mr T's NQT/ECT support
@MrTs_NQTs

A smile is the best weapon for disarming the parent that strides across the playground towards you. Smile, keep open body language and greet them with a 'Good morning, how are you? Is everything OK?' Make parents feel that they are heard and have had their thoughts acknowledged.

Parents' evenings

When parents' evenings approach, it is important to remember that the parents will be nervous too. For some they may not have a great relationship with school themselves and they may be anxious about what you are going to tell them about their child. Having been a teacher and a parent at these meetings, I can assure you that there are nerves on both sides.

Here are some tips to help you to make the most of the meeting.

❯ Be polite and keep your body language open: Welcome the parent into the room with a smile and the offer of a handshake and make eye contact. Guide them to where they will sit and, if in doubt, discuss the weather to put them at ease.

❯ Think about your seating (and its position): Avoid having a seat of power by you and the parents having the same type of chair. If, when you are sat down, you tower over the parents, you are instantly creating a power dynamic that may put some parents instantly on edge. Also, don't use a desk as a barrier; try to sit side by side rather than across a desk. This helps to create a feeling of equality for all. (Remember that some parents may have a lot of 'hang ups' from their own school experience; it is important that they feel at ease and valued in the discussion – more on this later.) When positioning the meeting space in the classroom, make sure that you can always see the door, and try to avoid the parents blocking your exit from the classroom, just in case. It allows you to seek support if you need it without the parents having to move. It also allows you to keep an eye on the door to see when the next parents arrive.

> Keep to time: This is one of those 'easier said than done' tips! Some parents will feel that being at a parents' evening is like a night out away from the kids and may be reluctant to head home. It is important for you to make sure that you get home at a reasonable hour and, for other waiting parents, that you stick to time as much as possible. Some schools may ring a bell every ten minutes, but most don't. Keeping sight of a clock will help. I always used to move it to the wall behind where the parent was sat so that I could see it. Sometimes I would put my watch on the desk. Most parents respect the timeframe for the meeting, but some will want to take up residence in your classroom. After the third time of hearing about how the parent is recovering from a bladder infection, saying 'Thank you so much for coming', whilst standing up and holding out your hand for a handshake, is enough to get most parents up and out. Some will continue the conversation standing up, in which case slowly start moving to the door to help to usher them out. On the other hand, there may be something important that does need to be discussed in more detail – then it would be good practice to say something along the lines of 'I can see that this is going to take longer than ten minutes for us to discuss properly. Let's make an appointment to talk again so that we can give it the time it needs.' Most parents will respect that and you can then give them the time without clock-watching.

> Find out what they want to know early on: Most parents just come to hear what you have to say. I always start by thanking them for coming and then asking, 'Do you have any particular questions or areas that you wanted to discuss this evening?' Most parents will respond with, 'No, I just want to know how they are getting on', at which point you can launch into the points that you wanted to discuss. However, if they do have specific queries, it means that you can get their priorities addressed early on, rather than you speaking for ten minutes to find that they then whip out a notebook full of questions. Parents should always have the opportunity to respond and discuss areas as they are raised, but getting their concerns and questions addressed first will ensure that they walk away knowing what they came to find out.

> Be prepared: If there is specific support or activities that you would like parents to do with their children at home, have the resources there ready. It gives you time to talk the parents through them so that they can get the

most out of the resources. Parents naturally want to support their children but they don't always have the confidence to do it in the 'right' way.

> Never give *that* parent the last slot: There will be the one parent who feels that by aiming for the last slot of the session they have you captive! Always try to put someone else after them to help them keep to time. If you have control of the timetabling of the slots, you may want to carefully consider where you place each parent. You may need to put separated families on different nights, you may want to spread out the more challenging parents or you may want to get them all done in the one evening. Planning carefully can help.

> Let the head know when your challenging parents are booked in: Headteachers can be very good at 'just popping in' to bring you a drink or a biscuit at key points. If there is a parent that you are concerned about, speak to the head about coordinating the two events. Just knowing that they are popping in – you can smile if things are going OK or invite them to sit down if you do need support – can give you a greater feeling of confidence.

> Keep notes private: If you make notes or want to share test scores or predicted grades with parents, write them down in a notebook for each child on their own page. Parents are eagle-eyed and want to know how their child compares to others. Minimise this by not having a class list with everyone's information on and by only having their child's information visible.

> Parents often hear what they want to: I never forget sitting with a parent and saying, 'Your child is not keeping up with where we'd like him to be at this point in the year. He is becoming more confident with reading, but cannot recognise enough sounds to be able to move on to the next reading band. In maths, he can confidently recognise numbers to 10 but at this point in the year we would like him to be able to recognise numbers to 20 confidently. He has some brilliant ideas in his writing, but is reluctant to record his ideas, and because he is not secure with enough sounds, he can find it hard to communicate in his writing.' The parent's response was, 'So he's doing OK, then?' I was in a job share at this point; we just looked at each other in disbelief. Perhaps we had been too positive; perhaps we had not reinforced clearly the expectations for the end of Year 1. Most parents want to hear how well their child is doing, and sometimes this is all that they focus on. If you need to deliver a challenging message about a child's progress, make sure that you do celebrate what they can do, but have those support materials on hand to guide parents in how they can help with the gaps. I am an eternal optimist and always want to start with the positives. However, I found it helpful to summarise at the end with a few key points beneficial to reinforcing the areas that the children were finding challenging – for example, 'He is doing really well with his maths, but if you could use these flash cards with him at home to help him to develop his sight vocabulary, it would really help, and we can start to get him back on track with his reading.'

Parents' evening is an opportunity to celebrate what the children can do, but also for parents to share their thoughts and concerns. There will be some children's parents who you will meet for the first time that evening, so using the time as wisely as you can is important. There may be some parents with whom you need to invest more time.

Structured conversations

I have always found that for parents of pupils with SEND or for pupils whom you want to find out a bit more about, structured conversations can be a great way forward. Structured conversations were part of the now dissolved Department for Children, Schools and Families' (DCSF) 'Achievement for all' agenda. The intention was that these meetings would happen for key parents instead of the traditional parents' evenings. Although an older piece of guidance, structured conversations still have value in providing relevant and effective support.

The purpose of the structured conversation, as outlined in The National Strategies document 'Achievement for all' (DCSF, 2009), is to:

> 'establish an effective relationship between parent and the key teacher;

> allow the parent an opportunity to share their concerns and, together, agree their aspirations for their child;

> set clear goals and targets for learning and improvement in wider outcomes;

> determine activities which will contribute to the achievement of those targets;

> identify the responsibilities of the parent, the pupil and the school;

> agree the date and time of the next meeting;

> clarify the most effective means of communication between meetings.

Perhaps most importantly, the structured conversation should help to establish a wider school culture of listening to the thoughts and aspirations of parents of young people with SEND. In short: 'receiving' as well as 'transmitting' information.

If these purposes are achieved then parents should:

> feel more confident to engage with their child's school;

> be given opportunities to contribute to their child's learning, express their views and concerns and be confident they will be acted upon;

> develop appropriately challenging expectations of what their child can achieve.

Schools should:

> be more effective at listening to parents about their child's learning;

> provide better information to parents about their child's learning;

❯ use the outcomes of the conversation with parents and pupils to improve the learning and teaching for individual targeted pupils.'

(DCSF, 2009, p. 4)

The structured conversation has a clear four-part structure:

❯ **Explore:** Actively listening to the parent, establishing an agreed understanding of the child.

❯ **Focus:** Identifying and clarifying key priorities for the pupil (and sometimes the family).

❯ **Plan**: What needs to happen? Agree the targets and how they will be addressed and by whom.

❯ **Review:** Summarise the discussion and the outcomes and establish future methods of communication.

These meetings can be time-consuming, and the biggest challenge can be finding the time to have them, but they are hugely productive. As teachers, it is important that we develop our active listening skills.

Active listening is about creating equity in the discussion by checking your understanding of what the parent means. Paraphrasing back can be a hugely powerful way of doing this – phrases like, 'So what you are saying is…, am I right?' and 'I can see how… would make you feel…, what do you feel would help the situation?'. Active listening is worth exploring for your own development; it will make you a better teacher, but also a better leader in the future.

COACHING MOMENT

▶ Where in your classroom would be the best place to host the parents?

▶ What key messages do you need to give?

▶ Can you say something positive about each child, or is there something that you know about the child beyond the academic that you can share with parents?

▶ What system will you use to keep to time?

▶ Will you make notes beforehand? If so, what are the most important things that you want the parents to know? What do they want to know?

▶ Are there any parents whom you have concerns about meeting? If yes, seek support from the SLT.

Mr T's NQT/ECT support
@MrTs_NQTs

Daily tip

Your reports should not contain any revelations for the parents; this is not the time to say you think their child is dyslexic. See it as the chance to reinforce the conversations you have already had this year.

Reports

End of term/end of year reports always arrive at a time when your workload is high and often when you are exhausted. However, they are the written snapshot of a pupil's time with you and will be proudly retained by parents for years to come.

Every school will have its own template for how reports are collated, but below are some tips and strategies to help you to complete these as effectively as possible.

■ General comments

Start with the general comments. Having been both the parent reading the report and the teacher writing it, I can honestly say that the general comment about the personal attributes and attitudes of a child is where every parent will look first – they want to see that you know their child. By starting with these personal attributes and attitudes first, when you are at your freshest, you will get the best out of the comments. This is the structure that I always used:

> **An overview statement:** Charlie has had a great, enjoyable, fantastic year in Emerald Class.

> **A personality trait comment**: She is a well-liked and sociable member of the class and contributes well to class discussions.

> **An overview of progress:** Charlie has made pleasing/great/fantastic progress this year and I have been especially pleased with how she has achieved in her reading.

> **An area of interest for them:** Charlie has shown a real enthusiasm for music this year and has readily been willing to join in with class singing.

> **A memorable moment:** Her performance in the Easter show was a huge moment of pride for Charlie and us all.

> **An area with which they may need more support:** Next year, Charlie will need to continue to develop her skills in mental maths. She has now mastered the times tables needed for Year 2, but these have not always come easily to her. In Year 3 she will need to use the strategies that she has developed this year to continue to build her mental maths skills.

> **A closing statement:** It has been a real pleasure to have Charlie in the class this year. I will miss her smile and cheery hello every morning and I wish her all the best for Year 3.

Less positive comments

For pupils who have not had such a positive year as 'Charlie' above, it is still important that we find the positives where we can. The language that we use is crucial:

> **For pupils who have not met expectations, focus on progress:** Sam has made pleasing progress this year. Whilst he has not yet met the age-related expectations for Year 5, he has secured many skills that will support him as he moves into Year 6.

> **Pupils who do not always give their full effort:** Finlay has achieved well this year, but with greater effort he could have achieved even more. Or, Chris does not always find it easy to focus in sessions and can be easily distracted by those around him.

> **For *those* pupils:** Alex has a lively personality and sometimes this can inhibit his ability to focus in class, and at times can cause issues in socialising with others.

Curriculum subjects

For curriculum subjects, always focus on the child's position in relation to the age-related expectations. Share their strengths in this subject and an area that needs further development, as well as how they could achieve it:

> **Curriculum-based comments:** Cody has not always found PE easy this year but has given her full effort in every session. She has mastered the basic skills needed in Year 4, and as she heads into Year 5 she will need to work on developing game tactics to help her and her team to be successful.

I always found that after writing the personal/general comments for every child, I was then able to go back to each child and focus on completing their entire report, as the general comments helped me to get immersed in a specific child. However, I had colleagues who would complete the English section for each child, then the maths, then the science and so on, as they found that this helped them to word things in a comparative way for pupils in order to reflect on their achievement. You will find your own way that works for you.

Remember to proofread – twice! I always avoided copying and pasting to prevent the gender pronoun issues that this can cause. Every year I presented my reports to the head to read and add comments to, and only one year did I manage to get no typos back. Mostly it was an 'an' instead of an 'and', but I always wanted the parents to feel that I had taken the time to get it right for their child.

COACHING MOMENT

▶ What does your school expect in terms of quantity and content of school reports?

▶ Before writing reports, can you articulate the strengths and areas for development for your pupils?

▶ What do you know about the pupils beyond their academic achievements?

Thoughts from an ECT

After years of working as an unqualified teacher, I am now currently working as an ECT in a special school. Prior to my training in 2016, if I had been approached to write this, it would have been very difficult. Why? Maybe, as I was naive and a little ignorant, I did not understand the magnitude of the importance of positive parental relationships. I feel that I was wrong, and I am now eternally grateful to those who challenged my views and helped me to develop and re-evaluate my ideas and opinions. I now truly understand the importance of working together with the parents.

World Book Day: all of my pupils and I were so excited to dress up as our favourite character, expect for one pupil. I observed that the child became anxious, and I identified that their body language was different. Despite my reassurance, I still felt that the child would go home feeling anxious. I rang to speak to the parents and explained; they said that it was evident that the child wanted to be involved, and the parent needed support. As a school, we offered anything possible to support the child: to bring their costume in rather than wear it, to provide a costume – anything that we could do to best support the pupil.

First, we devised a plan of how we could best support the child in making a significant change to a routine that they were heavily reliant on. It was decided that the best way to support the pupil was to create personalised Social Stories™ and a visual timetable of what we would wear on each day. On Wednesday: uniform; Thursday: uniform; and Friday: World Book Day costume. The class team and I dedicated time every day to discuss and read through the Social Story™. The pupil's parents would do the same at home and I would liaise with them throughout, to ensure that this was working and consider whether we needed to change or adapt our approach.

It is such a great feeling when your pupils achieve something: seeing them dressed up in their costume with a beaming smile on their face, proud of what they have achieved. I received an emotional email from the dad of the child saying thank you, and this was something that they had achieved for the first time, something that they did not think possible, and it is only by working together that we helped their child to achieve this.

Needless to say, World Book Day was a special day – a day that will stay with me forever.

I hope that this shows what is possible when you work together. Whilst the above story is successful and emphasises the importance of parent partnership, I have still made mistakes, such as forgetting to send letters home, but I am just honest and apologise. Working together with parents is not just about attending parents' evening; make sure when you are communicating with the parents/carers that it is not just about the negatives. I will always remember a parent answering a phone saying 'What have they done?', as the child's previous school had only rung when there was a negative incident at school. Relationships like this do not work and will break down very quickly. To help pupils to fulfil their potential, partnership with parents is paramount.

A mentor of mine says: Always remember that parents are the experts when it comes to their child.

Dan Archer, SENDECT

Key takeaways

- Building positive relationships with parents can pay dividends when you need their support.

- Be honest with parents and seek their perspective as much as possible.

- Utilise key strategies with parents when trying to engage them in discussions about their children.

- When communicating, be honest but supportive – what is going well, what needs to be developed and how.

- Parents want to see that you know their child and that you both have the child's best interests at heart.

CHAPTER 13

WHERE NEXT?

 Mr T's NQT/ECT support **Daily tip**
@MrTs_NQTs

As an ECT approaching the end of your second year, your final
assessment will be due! Make sure you have your voice heard by
filling in the box for your comments. Do you agree with the report?
What opportunities have you had? What are your aspirations for
next year?

        ♡

In this chapter we will:

➡ Reflect on where you are now in your ECT career.

➡ Celebrate the developments and impact that you have made.

➡ Consider where you want your career path to take you.

As a trainee and ECT, sometimes the focus can be getting through the next lesson, day, week or half-term. But at some point it is worth pausing and purposefully considering where you want your career to go. You may still not be sure at the time of reading this, but hopefully this chapter will help.

Where have you been?

If you are reading this, you have either read through and reached this chapter or you are here because you are now starting to think about where you want your career to go next. Either way, before we look forward, it is important to look back.

■ Are you in the right place?

When securing your first ECT post, the excitement of getting a job is often the most important factor. Sometimes when you work in a school, you may feel that it isn't the right environment for you to thrive in. That doesn't mean that it wouldn't be right for someone else though. If your current school is the school for you, then you may see your career path there. If not, it is worth using the time, before the jobs start appearing, to prioritise what you want from a school. Is it single-form entry? Parallel year group classes? A small rural school? A large urban school? The list of variations in school demographics and set-ups is near endless, but sometimes you will know what you don't want. That can be as good a starting point as any. The list of priorities/things to avoid can help you to shape the search for your next job. For me in my first position, I was in the right school, but I had been on a maternity contract and there were four NQTs on fixed-term contracts and only three permanent positions available, so I had to reapply for my own job. It also meant that one of us would not get a post, and these were now people that I considered friends. This was hugely challenging, and I remember the headteacher walking into my classroom at the end of the day to confirm that I had secured a post, and feeling a wave of relief, followed quickly by a feel of dread for who had been made redundant.

■ What have you enjoyed teaching?

As a trainee, we specialise in specific subjects through the route that we choose or the dissertation that we write at the end of our training. My specialism was maths, but I have never led maths as a subject in school. Sometimes this is about opportunities; sometimes it is about what you have an interest in. My first curriculum responsibility was PE. The PE coordinator left and I was finishing my NQT year and had enjoyed teaching PE, so I went for it! It was the best decision that I could have made. I had the opportunity for lots of CPD and to drive forward change in an often – at the time – neglected subject. My question to you is what subject have you enjoyed? What was your specialism? Would the opportunity be there for you to lead the subject next year? In the final term, my NQTs/ECTs always had time to shadow a curriculum leader in an area in which they had an interest. It helped them to develop an understanding of the role, and often led to a smooth handover of curriculum responsibility. As you move through your ECT induction, seek out opportunities to do the same – ask your mentor to arrange a time for you to meet with the subject lead, to begin to build your understanding of the role, before taking on the responsibility when you are asked or when you are ready. (Remember that it doesn't have to be an area in which you specialised but perhaps instead an area in which you feel that you could make an impact.)

What impact have you made on the children?

Before the pupils leave, look at the first and last pieces of work in their books. Recognise the journey that they have been on and your key role in that. Regardless of the year group or subject that you are teaching, there would have been highs and lows. By looking at the pupils' work, it can give you tangible evidence of your impact on their education. Also consider what impact the children have made on you. What skills have you developed because of working with these pupils? Has your knowledge of specific needs been developed? Have you refined a teaching style that works for you? Do you now have some 'go to' strategies to support pupils or introduce new content? It is also worth considering whether the age of pupils has suited you and whether you have suited them. I have loved working with every age group that I have taught and found things that I enjoyed teaching about all of them. I do remember being petrified of heading into Reception to teach. However, I loved teaching this year group, but for very different reasons to why I enjoyed teaching Year 6. There may be a year group that you feel would suit you better. That is OK. Speak to your headteacher – we all have our strengths and skillsets that lend themselves to working with specific groups of pupils; by matching these together, we get the best out of both.

What impact have you made on the wider school?

As an ECT, you might be offered opportunities that you feel you can't say no to (see Chapter 4), but hopefully the ones that you have said yes to have allowed you to get a sense of the wider school and its community. I remember in my NQT year being at the summer fete and being in the stocks whilst the kids chucked wet sponges at me. (Some four-year-olds have a mean aim!) This allowed me to gain a sense of community and to build relationships that meant that when I became English lead a few years later, when I asked the PTA to fund new reading books the money was there! I also had the opportunity to develop and lead a tennis club after school for pupils. Both of these allowed me to develop my own skills and added to any future applications to show how I could contribute beyond the classroom. What opportunities have you had? What impact have you contributed to the wider school?

■ What impact has the school had on you?

I remember vividly at the end of my NQT year feeling very at home and settled in my school. I had developed a good relationship with the staff, pupils and parents and felt that it was a school in which I could thrive. However, I also remember thinking about how much I had developed and changed as a teacher. I had worked with a child with complex learning needs (something that I had not experienced in my training). My values around education had shifted. I could see the impact of the positive relationships that I had formed with colleagues, pupils and parents, and developing the sense that teaching was not about me looking good doing it; it was about the impact that I was having on pupils. I trained during the time of the numeracy and literacy strategy, so every lesson looked identical in structure, but I was beginning to see the benefits of alternative structures to my lessons. I had worked in a parallel Year 2 class and my pupils had performed equally well in their SATs as my colleague's class. And I had been through my first Ofsted and felt buoyed by the feedback that I had been given (I had a newfound sense of confidence that I knew what I was doing). I am an introvert at heart, but I had stood up in front of parents and led an assembly, as well as feeding back to colleagues about a training course that I had been on – both huge things for me. How has your school changed you as a teacher? Have you found your tribe or are you still looking?

COACHING MOMENT

► What have you enjoyed most this year?

► What do you feel that your strengths are as a teacher?

► What is the biggest impact that you have had this year?

► How have you been changed by your school?

Mr T's NQT/ECT support
@MrTs_NQTs

Daily tip

As you move towards the end of induction, start to think about your strengths and where you want them to take you in the next five years. Is there a subject you want to lead? Do you want to be a phase or year group lead? An assistant or deputy head? Now is a good time to shadow and develop an understanding of what the roles entail.

Celebrate

This chapter is one for you to review as you approach the end of your ECT induction. It is important that you take time to celebrate and recognise the development in you as a teacher during this time. This section will be focused on prompting you to reflect, rather than giving you tips.

> Reflect on that first day or your first lesson. Consider the teacher that you were then – how have you changed?

> What are your lessons like now?

> What are the values that drive you? Are they still the same as when you first started or have they changed?

> Have you become the sort of teacher that you wanted to be?

> What are the best bits of feedback that you have received from a child, a colleague and a parent?

> What have you learned that will influence what you do next year? Are there some key aspects to your classroom that you want to develop? Are there key teaching strategies that you want to develop?

> Who in your current school inspires you? What have you learned from them?

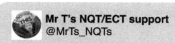 

Mr T's NQT/ECT support
@MrTs_NQTs

During your induction, you may start to develop a passion for a subject or aspect of school life. Speak to your mentor about further CPD and opportunities. It may even become an area that you can lead in the future.

Next steps in your career

As you approach the end of your induction, you may need to start making more conscious choices about how and where you want your career to progress. Where do you see yourself in five years' time? Perhaps as a SENDCo, a year leader or a deputy head? You may want to study a Master's degree. I did my Master's degree three years into my teaching (it took me four years to complete), but at that point in my career I did not have a huge number of additional responsibilities, so had the time to focus on my studies. At the start of my career, national professional qualifications (NPQs) and the National Professional Qualification for Middle Leadership (NPQML) didn't exist, but they may be worth serious consideration for you for the coming years if you want to achieve a deputy headship in five years' time. These are not things to be undertaken during induction, but having the conversations with your mentor/headteacher about their willingness to support you with these may be. This is particularly true if you are considering moving schools – it may help you with your decision.

At the time of writing this book, there is a new wave of NPQs for those looking towards middle leadership opportunities:

> **Leading Teacher Development:** For teachers who have, or are aspiring to have, responsibilities for leading the development of other teachers in their school.

> **Leading Teaching:** For teachers who have, or are aspiring to have, responsibilities for leading teaching in a subject, year group, key stage or phase.

> **Leading Behaviour and Culture:** For teachers who have, or are aspiring to have, responsibilities for leading behaviour or supporting pupil wellbeing in their school.

> **Leading Literacy:** For teachers who have, or are aspiring to have, responsibilities for leading literacy across a school, year group, key stage or phase.

> **Early Years Leadership:** For leaders qualified to at least level 3 with a full and relevant qualification, who are, or are aspiring to be:
>   ○ managers of private, voluntary and independent nurseries
>   ○ headteachers of school-based or maintained nurseries
>   ○ childminders with leadership responsibilities.

After this, there are NPQs for:

> **Senior Leadership:** For school leaders who are, or are aspiring to be, a senior leader with cross-school responsibilities.

> **Headship:** For school leaders who are, or are aspiring to be, a headteacher or head of school with responsibility for leading a school.

> **Executive Leadership:** For school leaders who are, or are aspiring to be, an executive headteacher or to have a school trust CEO role with responsibility for leading several schools.

The middle leadership NPQs are currently (at the time of writing this) being funded by the DfE. However, there is a cost to schools for your supply cover to attend training. If one of these areas interests you, it could definitely be worth having the conversation.

For me, being the best teacher that I could be was my career goal for the first five years – to be good at what I did and to know that the children in my care had the best opportunity to achieve their full potential. Undertaking a Master's degree supported me with this, as well as the reading and CPD opportunities that I sought out. (School budgets were not as stretched then, so CPD was a priority for staff – and it still should be!) Your ECT induction can be used to give you a head start at this. Ask your mentor to organise visits to other schools during your ECT time to help you to diversify your teaching strategies. Utilise social media and teacher networks to 'magpie' ideas and begin to build your teaching toolkit early on. Every time you try something new, you will learn from it and it will shape you as a teacher. Without getting too cheesy, teachers are grown and not made. Nobody arrives as the finished article; we all have a journey that develops and shapes us into who we are and who we want to be. Sometimes we seek out opportunities; sometimes opportunities find us. If it is the right opportunity for you, go for it and grab it. If it is not the right path for you, then be brave enough to decline.

The Master's degree that I chose was in inclusive education. I chose this because, over my time in the school in which I taught, I had developed a passion and enthusiasm for working with pupils with SEND. At the time at which I started my Master's degree, the National Award for SEN

Co-ordination did not exist, but had it have done, this would have given me the opportunity to start on that pathway. I never did hold the role of SENDCo; my career went down a different path and led me to assistant and then deputy headship. But SEND is still an area for which I have a huge passion!

The reason for sharing this with you is that I get asked quite frequently on Twitter whether teachers should start a Master's degree. Questions are often about the timing and the subject. This is such a personal thing. I started mine three years in and was grateful for that, as I had a good grasp of the day job so could give my Master's the focus that it needed without impacting my workload hugely. However, I did lose many holidays to writing assignments and research. You will know your circumstances and when the right time for you will be. I chose the subject of my Master's degree because I was genuinely interested in it, and it also would have supported me with where I thought my career would go. Out of these two reasons, the fact that it was an area of interest was definitely the reason that kept me going when it got tough!

Another question that I get asked a lot is about leadership opportunities that arise in schools during or towards the end of induction. The question is usually around 'Should I go for it?' or 'Do I have enough experience?'. My answer is always the same. If you feel ready for it, then go for it. Walk into the role with your eyes open and find out as much as you can beforehand, but if you feel that it is the right time for you, then you have nothing to lose. Plus it shows ambition and a want to contribute to the school beyond your classroom. Experience is a strange thing for me; a measure of time is not the same as a measure of experience. This was epitomised for me when a new head arrived at the school at which I was deputy head. During the February half-term, he said to me that he had been in education for 16 years and had experienced more in the last six months than he had during the previous 15 and a half years. Just because you have only taught for eight months, 12 months or two years, it does not mean that you don't have the experience that you need. As I said, if you feel ready for it – go for it!

Your ECT induction is just the start of your journey to becoming the best teacher that you can be. It can give you the foundations on which to build your career. Sometimes you will know exactly where you want to be and the route to get there. At other times you may take a convoluted route and suddenly realise that your career has turned out differently to how you anticipated. As long as you are happy with what you have achieved, never compare your journey to others and always be grateful for the opportunities that you have had.

COACHING MOMENT

▶ What do you enjoy the most? Is it teaching or is it more strategic work?

▶ What subjects do you feel passionate about?

▶ Where do you feel that you could make the biggest impact going forward?

Thoughts from an ECT

Often as an ECT you can be surrounded by lots of talk about career progression, with some people pushing you forward and some saying that you're too young or need more experience. I began teaching as a supply during the pandemic, but by October had secured a position for the year at a school working part-time. After the first year, I was offered a full-time contract, which has become a permanent contract. I believe in taking opportunities as they arise, and although at first I would have loved a permanent full-time job straight away, this school's context was exactly where I wanted to work and I had a gut feeling that this would work out, much like it has. I set my ambitions high, with the focus on mathematics lead. I think that it is important to consider why you want career progression and how you're currently managing your time and responsibilities before jumping ahead. For me, I love mathematics and could see how I could help our school to progress within this topic. I specialised in mathematics at university and have always enjoyed the subject, making it concrete, practical and accessible to each individual child.

I had not set a goal that by the end of my ECT I must become a 'lead teacher'; I was focused on using my skills and passion for mathematics to help our school. If this is your motivation for progression, I think it is always the right time and to go for it. I don't believe in setting a structured 'career progression map', as this can cause unnecessary pressure and mean that you may take roles or positions that you are not passionate about.

To help with the steps I have made in my career so far, I have studied at Master's level whilst teaching. Whilst this is by no means necessary, I have found it extremely helpful and rewarding to design my research programme around my interests in school. This year I am currently working on an NPQLT to develop my leadership skills, to help build my confidence in supporting more experienced members of staff with mathematics, as this is my passion.

I believe the best way to approach career progression is to find your route. There are no golden rules or lists of instructions for you to follow. It is all about finding the right route for you. I would advise that you find a school where you fit, where you feel supported and where you enjoy working. Then use the support of those around you; tell your mentors and senior leadership team your goals and passions, and take every opportunity that comes your way. Most importantly, don't put yourself down or hold yourself back for fear of age or experience. Our headteacher sends out a question to each member of staff asking what year group you'd like to teach and what subject you would like to lead. I answered this honestly, with the hope that I could lead maths but with no expectation, assuming that I would need more experience. The school gave me that role with the support of the previous mathematics lead, to support me as an early career teacher. They trusted in my ability more than I did originally. In my experience, if your leadership team is calling on you for a role, it is because they believe in you and know that you can perform in a way that moves the school forward.

Sarah Robson, Secondary ECT

Key takeaways

- Celebrate everything that you have achieved during your induction – you should be hugely proud.
- Sometimes we need to seek out opportunities in order to make the next steps in our career happen; sometimes we need to grasp the opportunities that come along.
- Your career is your own – be brave and go for it!

GLOSSARY (ALSO KNOWN AS ACRONYM OVERLOAD!)

ADD: Attention deficit disorder

ADHD: Attention deficit hyperactivity disorder

AfL: Assessment for learning – a set of principles for assessing pupils during lessons

ASC/D: Autism spectrum condition/disorder

AST: Advanced Skills Teacher – a teacher with a specialism that is often employed to support schools

ATS: Advisory Teaching Service – an external agency that can provide additional support for specific pupils

CAMHS: Child and Adolescent Mental Health Services

CYPMHS: Children and Young People's Mental Health Service

DDSL: Deputy designated safeguarding lead

DSL:	Designated safeguarding lead
ECF:	Early Career Framework
ECT:	Early career teacher
Ed psych/EP:	Educational psychologist
EHCP:	Education, health and care plan
EYFS:	Early Years Foundation Stage
G+T:	Gifted and talented
IEP:	Individual education plan
LAC/CLA:	Looked after child/child looked after – a term for a child who is currently in the care system or living with other relatives under a special guardianship order
LADO:	Local Authority Designated Officer (safeguarding)
MAT:	Multi-academy trust
MFL:	Modern foreign languages
NLE:	National Leader of Education – a headteacher who is recognised for their school-to-school support work
NPQ:	National professional qualifications – these are DfE-recognised qualifications in professional development; there are various levels (see Chapter 13 for details)
NQT:	Newly qualified teacher
PDA:	Pathological demand avoidance
PPA:	Planning, preparation and assessment time
PRU:	Pupil referral unit

PSHE: Personal, social and health education (subject to change – frequently)

Pupil Premium: This is additional funding for certain qualifying pupils. Pupils qualify for this additional funding if: they are currently, or have been eligible for free school meals in the last six years; they are in the care system or have been adopted from care; they have parents in the armed forces. The amount of funding varies depending on which category they fall into. If pupils fit more than one category, they are only eligible for the highest-value funding.

RAP: Raising attainment plan

RSE: Relationships and sex education

SaLT: Speech and language therapist

SEF: Self-evaluation form (an overview of the school for Ofsted)

SEMH: Social, emotional and mental health

SEND: Special educational needs and disability

SENDCo: Special educational needs and disability coordinator

SLE: Specialist leader in education – a teacher with a specialism that is often employed to support schools

SpLD: Specific learning disability

Feel free to use the space below to keep track of the acronyms/terminology that are particular to your school:

REFERENCES

ADHD Collective (2017), 'What does it feel like to have ADHD?'. Available at: https://adhdcollective.com/what-does-it-feel-like-to-have-adhd

Bandura, A. (1977), *Social Learning Theory*. Englewood Cliffs, NJ: Prentice Hall.

BBC (2018), 'Shopping through the eyes of someone with autism', BBC News. Available at: www.bbc.co.uk/news/av/uk-45762016

Black, P. and Wiliam, D. (1998), *Inside the Black Box: Raising Standards Through Classroom Assessment*. London: nferNelson.

Cuddy, A. (2012), 'Your body language may shape who you are', TED Talk. Available at: www.youtube.com/watch?v=Ks-_Mh1QhMc

Department for Children, Schools and Families (DCSF) (2009), 'Achievement for all: The structured conversation: Handbook to support training'. Available at: https://dera.ioe.ac.uk/2418

Department for Education (DfE) (2012), 'Induction appeals procedures'. Available at: www.gov.uk/government/publications/induction-appeals-procedures

Department for Education (DfE) (2013), 'The national curriculum in England: Primary curriculum'. Available at: www.gov.uk/government/publications/national-curriculum-in-england-primary-curriculum

Department for Education (DfE) (2016) 'School workforce in England: November 2015', National statistics. Available at: https://assets.publishing.service.gov.uk/government/uploads/system/uploads/attachment_data/file/533618/SFR21_2016_MainText.pdf

Department for Education (DfE) (2019), 'Early career framework'. Available at: www.gov.uk/government/publications/early-career-framework

Department for Education (DfE) (2020), 'Assessment framework: Reception baseline assessment'. Available at: https://assets.publishing.service.gov.uk/government/uploads/system/uploads/attachment_data/file/868099/2020_Assessment_Framework_Reception_Baseline_Assessment.pdf

Department for Education (DfE) (2021), 'Induction for early career teachers (England)'. Available at: https://assets.publishing.service.gov.uk/government/uploads/system/uploads/attachment_data/file/972316/Statutory_Induction_Guidance_2021_final__002_____1___1_.pdf

Department for Education (DfE) (2022), 'Guidance for early career teachers (ECTs): ECF-based training'. Available at: www.gov.uk/guidance/guidance-for-early-career-teachers-ects-ecf-based-training#you-do-not-need-to-collect-evidence

Department for Education (DfE) and Department of Health and Social Care (DHSC) (2015), 'SEND code of practice: 0 to 25 years'. Available at: www.gov.uk/government/publications/send-code-of-practice-0-to-25

Dix, P. (2017), *When the Adults Change, Everything Changes: Seismic shifts in school behaviour.* Bancyfelin, Carmarthen: Independent Thinking Press.

Education Endowment Foundation (EEF) (2018), 'Making best use of teaching assistants'. Available at: https://educationendowmentfoundation.org.uk/education-evidence/guidance-reports/teaching-assistants

Glasser, W. (1997), '"Choice theory" and student success'. *The Education Digest*, 63, (3), 16.

Martin-Denham, S. (2015), *Teaching Children & Young People with Special Educational Needs & Disabilities.* London: SAGE.

Standards and Testing Agency (STA) (2018), 'Teacher assessment frameworks at the end of Key Stage 1'. Available at: https://assets.publishing.service.gov.uk/government/uploads/system/uploads/attachment_data/file/740343/2018-19_teacher_assessment_frameworks_at_the_end_of_key_stage_1_WEBHO.pdf

The Understood Team (2016), 'A day in the life of a teen with dyscalculia'. Available at: https://tinyurl.com/y5vmverf

Wiliam, D. (2015), 'Questioning'. Available at: www.youtube.com/watch?v=y8bHMd3PosM

Williams, N. (2015), 'What is it like to have dyspraxia?', The Blog With (More Than) One Post. Available at: https://theblogwithonepost.wordpress.com/2015/01/17/31

INDEX